Ghostly Cries From Dixie

Pat Fitzhugh

THE ARMAND PRESS
NASHVILLE

The names of the people and places discussed in this book are a product of the author's research, which he believed to be accurate to the best of his knowledge at the time of publication. The stories contained in this book come from history, folklore, and modern eyewitness accounts. This book contains factual *and* fictional elements.

Most locations discussed in this book are privately owned and should not be entered without prior permission from the respective owner(s). Merely reading this book does not constitute permission to enter any location mentioned in this book. If a location's owner gives you permission to enter the location, the author urges you to be careful and act responsibly. The author is not responsible for your actions or your personal safety. You are. The author's only role is to entertain you with ghost stories.

ISBN-10: 0-9705156-5-0
ISBN-13: 978-0-9705156-5-0

Printed in the United States of America

✍ CONTENTS ✑

❧ PREFACE ❧

F ROM THE DARK SWAMPS OF LOUISIANA TO THE MISTY HILLS AND HOLLOWS OF APPALACHIA, the American South is enshrouded by a mystical element that rouses the senses and kindles the imagination. For centuries, this mystical element has inspired tales of ghosts haunting old houses, creatures roaming the forests, and headless apparitions waving lanterns.

The region's supernatural mystique is traceable to its violent and bloody past, when disastrous accidents, bloody battles, sweeping epidemics, and brutal murders claimed countless lives and left behind a spiritual residue that lingers on. Nearly every old graveyard, long-standing house, and Civil War battlefield in the South has a resident spirit and a ghostly tale to tell.

I wrote this book for the many people who enjoy such tales. Each chapter contains my version of a particular ghost story. Although I've known the stories most of my life, I scoured libraries, newspapers, and other sources for more information to include. You are probably familiar with *some* of the stories, but read them anyway; stories often change when new information surfaces.

I kept three objectives in mind while writing this book. The first was to intrigue, fascinate, and entertain people. That's right—to entertain! Although a great deal of research went into this book, it remains a storybook.

My second objective was quality over quantity. Instead of stuffing this book with a multitude of short, watered-down stories to increase its page count, I cover fewer stories in more detail. This, I feel, gives the reader more insight. Longer stories add *depth and dimension to* a book. Simply proclaiming, "Junior saw a ghost, wet his pants, and ran like hell," doesn't tell the reader much.

My third objective was to strike a healthy balance between history and ghostlore. I have tried, wherever possible, to corroborate the stories with real events and historical data. As a historian – someone who studies history and shares their findings with others –, I feel that striking such a balance helps the reader to develop a greater appreciation for history and the sense of validity it can add to a ghost story.

History often proves the existence of a story's characters, but it doesn't always bear witness to the *events* alleged to have taken place. Andrew Jackson was real, but did he encounter an infamous witch? Where does one draw the line between fact and fiction? That's up to you.

I am dedicating this book to those who are intrigued, fascinated, and entertained by ghost stories. You are my audience – the people I write for, the people I run my websites for, the people I conduct my research for, and the people I like to meet when I am on the road doing lectures and book signings. My allegiance is to you.

I would like to thank my parents, Bob and Betty Fitzhugh, as well as my friends and family, for the unwavering support they have shown me over the years. I also would like to thank those who shared their personal ghost stories with me, and those who allowed me to use their photos in this book.

Come with me on a terrifying, mystical journey down the road less traveled, where ghosts, haints, and spirits stand a vigilant watch over cypress-filled swamps, forgotten graveyards, old houses, and majestic mountains. Pleasant dreams.

Pat Fitzhugh

✌ ONE ✎

Mayhem on the Mississippi

ONE OF THE MOST TRAGIC EVENTS IN CIVIL WAR HISTORY occurred on the Mississippi River, seven miles north of Memphis, Tennessee. The steamer *Sultana*, carrying 2,400 passengers, burst into a hellish inferno of molten steel, hot coals, and human carnage when her boiler exploded in the early morning hours of April 27, 1865.

Those pinned in the wreckage slowly burned to death, while others drowned in the frigid depths of the Mississippi. About 1,900 men, women, and children perished that fateful morning, and their restless spirits still linger at the disaster site. This is their story.

When the Civil War ended, the government offered to pay steamboat companies $5 for each Union soldier they carried home. Steamboat companies liked the idea because it allowed them to boost their profits by overloading their boats. Carrying 600 soldiers on a single boat would generate more profit than carrying 300 soldiers on two different boats would generate; an overloaded steamboat meant a healthier bottom line.

The 280-foot *Sultana* was the most profitable steamboat on the Mississippi. Equipped to carry only 376 passengers, she routinely transported soldiers in groups of 500 or more, and always arrived on time. Union Army officers were so impressed by her stellar performance that they solicited monetary kickbacks from her owner in exchange for their assigning more soldiers to ride her.

A contingent of 1,900 homeward bound Union soldiers gathered at Vicksburg, Mississippi on the morning of April 24, 1865 to await the Sultana's arrival from New Orleans. She had left the Crescent City three days earlier with 230 passengers and a cargo of sugar and cattle. Running more than six hours late, she slowly steamed into Vicksburg at 5:30 P.M. Her main boiler had malfunctioned downriver, which caused the delay.

While crewmembers repaired a large crack in the boiler, Union officers discussed the idea of squeezing all 1,900 soldiers into the Sultana. If they succeeded, their kickback would amount to almost $5,000. Boiler repairs were completed by 9 P.M., and the Sultana steamed away from Vicksburg with over 2,000 passengers.

When she docked at Helena, Arkansas two days later, onlookers noticed that she was listing (leaning) to her port (left) side. One onlooker was concerned enough to take a picture. The picture on the previous page, taken at Helena on April 26, 1865, shows the Sultana listing under the weight of more than 2,000 passengers.

After a brief stay in Helena, the overloaded Sultana chugged her way upriver to Memphis, Tennessee, where she arrived early that evening. A routine boiler inspection revealed another large crack, which required her to stay in Memphis until repairs could be made. Many soldiers went ashore and visited local taverns to pass the time. A drink and a leisurely stroll didn't seem like a bad idea; the battle-worn soldiers wouldn't be able to go ashore again until they reached Cairo, Illinois, some three days up the river. Meanwhile, over 200 more passengers boarded the Sultana, many of them women and children.

Crewmembers wound up the boiler repairs by 11 P.M., and the soldiers began returning to the vessel; a few were lucky enough to be left behind. At midnight, Captain J.C. Mason, the Sultana's 34-year-old master and part owner, gave the engine room a "steam up" order and sounded her whistle. The overstressed Sultana hissed, heaved, and slowly chugged off into the darkness.

Flooding in the Midwest had made the river's current much stronger than usual, and the Sultana – so weighted down with passengers that she could hardly move – was plying against the current. A lot of steam pressure was required in order to maintain her forward progression. She would also lose considerable time because a thick layer of fog had settled on the river after a late-evening downpour. A treacherous voyage lay ahead for the Sultana and her 2,400 weary passengers.

The lack of space aboard the overcrowded Sultana made it difficult for passengers to settle in for the evening. The wealthier passengers had staterooms to sleep in, but the soldiers were forced to make do with the outer decks. Children slept on the main deck, near the boiler room, because the heat from the boilers and the slow, repetitious straining sounds coming from the engines helped put them to sleep. Nearly every mother and child on board the Sultana that morning slept near the boiler room.

Navigating through heavy fog and laboring against the swift current, the Sultana had been underway for only two hours when she passed "The Chicken and Hens," a small cluster of islands seven miles north of Memphis. It was 2 A.M.; the coal oil streetlights back in Memphis had long since faded, and nothing but the dark, treacherous Mississippi River lay ahead. An eerie silence befell the Sultana as she plied through the dead of night, her passengers fast asleep.

Suddenly, a strong blast sent passengers flying over the deck rails and into the river. Some were killed by the impact of the blast; others suffered broken limbs and tried to stay afloat, but their badly maimed bodies soon proved to be no match for the river's fierce current. Their agonizing screams quickly turned into gurgling and choking sounds. Seconds later, a ghastly chorus of shrill, gut-wrenching screams came from the boiler room, which had become a stew of burning wood and molten steel.

One minute later, another blast jolted the Sultana, hurling a mixture of red-hot coals throughout the vessel and hurling burning bodies into the river. Fire spread rampantly. Chaos and panic ensued. The remaining passengers frantically rushed to the outer decks in hopes of avoiding the thickening smoke. Unfortunately, many couldn't move quickly enough because of their severe injuries; in some cases, other passengers helped them along.

In minutes, the Sultana had become a floating inferno of burning wood, molten steel, and charred human carnage, drifting aimlessly through the dead of night.

Several passengers jumped overboard and clung to floating driftwood, but the ice-cold water temperature brought on hypothermia. These would-be survivors were found five miles downstream the next morning, frozen to the very driftwood they had thought would save their lives. By daybreak, the once luxurious and dependable Sultana had been reduced to a bed of ashes; only 500 of her 2,400 passengers survived.

Authorities at Memphis had seen a bright glow in the night sky and formed a search party. Searchers found survivors clinging to bushes along the riverbank and took them to a Memphis hospital, where many later died from burn complications. Identifying bodies recovered from the river proved difficult because many victims had been burned beyond recognition or had been severely disfigured by the blasts. Other bodies had become entangled in submerged brush; wild animals found them two months later when the floodwaters receded.

The Sultana disaster claimed almost 2,000 lives, yet the tragedy received little news coverage. It's likely that the disaster was overshadowed by other newsworthy events of the period, such as Lee's surrender to Grant on April 9th, Abraham Lincoln's assassination on April 14th, and the capture of John Wilkes Booth on April 26th. However, the spiritual residue left behind by the Sultana tragedy has never been overshadowed; the disaster site is a treasure trove of supernatural activity that can be seen, heard, and even felt.

Always changing its course, the mighty Mississippi River now flows three miles east of the disaster site. The Sultana's remains rest twenty feet beneath a soybean field in eastern Arkansas.

For years, tugboat captains on the Mississippi River

have reported seeing a yellowish-orange mist glowing high above the field, usually late at night or in the early morning hours. The glow, which appears randomly and sometimes lasts until daybreak, resembles the glow emitted by a fire.

On a spring night in the late 1980's, a group of four local paranormal investigators set out to study the mysterious glow and investigate changes in temperature at the disaster site. Their investigation was based on the premise that a significant change in temperature would indicate the presence of a heat source.

Proving the existence of a heat source would help to debunk a popular theory that suggests the glowing mist comes from airborne luminescent chemicals. The investigators would document the temperature at the disaster site and nearby sites, and then try to match their data to the timeframe in which the glow appeared. An average of the temperature readings taken at nearby sites would form the baseline. A marked increase in temperature at the disaster site when the glow is present would suggest that the glow is related to a heat source as opposed to luminescent chemicals in the air.

The investigators first spotted the eerie glow when they came within a mile of the disaster site. They stopped their vehicle at that point and began their investigation. Equipped with an outdoor thermometer, a pedometer, and a walkie-talkie, two investigators walked toward the disaster site while the other investigators remained in their vehicle. When they reached the disaster site, they didn't see the glowing mist or anything out of the ordinary, but the field seemed much warmer than the area around it. Their thermometer registered a balmy eighty-six degrees.

They walked a half mile away from the disaster site and checked the temperature again. Their thermometer registered fifty-nine degrees, which was consistent with the local weather forecast. They radioed the other investigators, who checked the temperature at their location a mile away. Their thermometer, too, registered fifty-nine degrees. Oddly, from their vantage point, they could see the glowing mist looming over the disaster site; it had been visible the entire time.

The most important observation made by the investigators – even more important than the change in temperature – was the glowing mist. From a mile away, one team observed the glowing mist in the sky above the disaster site. At the same time, however, the team stationed *at* the disaster site saw nothing in the sky. Although data suggest the presence of a heat source, its origin remains a mystery.

Some researchers feel that the glowing mist and warm temperature at the disaster site are evidence of a *residual haunting*, in which lingering spiritual residue forces the disaster to replay itself. Evidence of a residual haunting at the site isn't limited to unusually warm temperatures and a fiery glow in the night sky, however. For years, people have heard ghastly sounds and seen horrific apparitions there.

Men hunting raccoons in the nearby woods late at night have heard cries, choking, gasping, and other deathly sounds coming from the disaster site. Interestingly, these ghastly sounds are usually heard when the glowing mist appears above the field. The combination of intense heat, a fiery glow, and scores of people fighting to stay alive describes perfectly the Sultana disaster. The disaster also has a terrifying sequel, which replays itself a few hours later.

People driving near the disaster site just after daybreak have seen disfigured, human-like figures walking standing the field and occasionally sifting the dirt. Clad in period clothing, the figures fade into the early morning fog after a few minutes. Paranormal researchers have theorized that the figures are the ghosts of Sultana victims who are perhaps trying to locate their lost belongings.

With so many years having passed, it's nearly impossible for one to understand the pain and agony felt by those who perished in the Sultana tragedy. The spiritual residue left behind serves as a constant reminder of what those 1,900 men, women, and children felt that dreadful morning.

It is disheartening to know that the disaster site, with its gruesome sounds and ghastly apparitions, is but a subtle reminder of a tragedy so big that it claimed more lives than the Titanic disaster claimed, yet because of scant news coverage, it will remain a mere footnote in the annals of American history.

✌ TWO ✌

Waverly Hills TB Sanatorium

ITUATED ATOP A WINDY HILL ON THE OUTSKIRTS OF Louisville, Kentucky is the abandoned Waverly Hills Tuberculosis Sanatorium building. Obscured by rolling hills, sprawling thickets, and random patches of ivy scaling its aging walls, the imposing brick structure was once a thriving, state-of-the-art treatment center for those who suffered the ravaging effects of tuberculosis.

Called the *White Plague* because its victims often appear pale, tuberculosis is a potentially fatal disease that usually attacks the lungs. It is contracted by inhaling the deadly *Mycobacterium Tuberculosis* bacteria present in air that is exhaled by infected persons. Symptoms of the highly contagious disease include fever, extreme fatigue, and coughing up blood. Tuberculosis moves from the lungs to other parts of the body during its latter stages, ultimately consuming the patient.

Public concern about the horrific disease mounted in the late 1800's when one in every five deaths was attributed to it. People of all ages and lifestyles succumbed to the disease in record numbers; young and middle-aged adults were the most susceptible. By 1900, Tuberculosis had become an epidemic in northern Kentucky. The low-lying wetlands along the Ohio River, ripe with stagnant air and swamp gas, made it easy for deadly bacteria to develop. Insects then carried the bacteria to urban areas.

In 1910, public health officials built Waverly Hills Tuberculosis Sanatorium, an institution-like facility where tuberculosis patients could be quarantined and treated. The original building, which housed only 50 patients, soon outgrew itself; it was replaced in 1926 by a larger building that still stands today. Waverly Hills treated its last tuberculosis patient in 1960.

When walking down the old building's dark hallways and peeking into its deserted rooms, one gets a sense of what Waverly Hills was like during its heyday. There were nurse's stations, operating rooms, recreation rooms, administrative offices, a morgue, a chapel, a library, and a large dining room. A large staff worked around the clock. Because Waverly Hills was a quarantine facility, all food consumed by its staff and patients was grown and processed there. Patient social activities included card games, parties, and classes. Sadly, the strong sense of hope that filled the air proved to be no match for the deadly bacteria that filled the air.

More than one-half of all tuberculosis patients died within three to five years of being diagnosed with the disease. Effective treatment and a potential cure wouldn't become available until the introduction of Streptomycin in 1946. Until then, the few available treatments, such as removing ribs and collapsing an infected lung, were risky and provided little hope.

Thousands of patients succumbed to the disease at Waverly Hills, and their souls still roam the building, forever in search of the cure they never lived to see.

Witnesses have spotted ghostly apparitions in nearly every part of the building, including patient rooms, the morgue, laboratories, recreation and dining areas, and even mechanical areas. Each area of the building seems to have a resident ghost.

One of the most prominent areas of Waverly Hills is the solarium porchway, where patient beds were arranged side-by-side and facing large open windows along a porch-like walkway. Doctors believed that the constant supply of fresh air would aid in the recovery process and help rid the hospital of contaminated air.

Apparitions of patients wearing 1930's-period hospital gowns often wander about the solarium porchway, even acknowledging each other on occasion. Confined to their own dimension in time, the apparitions are oblivious to our dimension (the present). Visitors occasionally hear moaning, coughing, and choking sounds coming from the abandoned patient rooms directly behind the solarium porchway. During the facility's heyday, those rooms housed the sanatorium's most critical patients.

The building's many long hallways are also home to ghostly activity. While touring the building, visitors have seen *shadow people* peek their heads out of doorways or suddenly dart across hallways. Most of these sightings occurred on the third and fourth floors, where children were treated. The shadow people aren't believed to be dangerous; some researchers think they are the ghosts of children playing hide-and-go-seek.

The fifth floor seems to be the most active floor at Waverly Hills, and most of the activity is attributable to the ghosts of two young nurses who committed suicide there on different occasions.

Many believe that a young nurse jumped out the window of patient room 502 back in the late 1920's. Since then, people have felt drastic temperature drops when entering the room. Using thermometers and other devices, paranormal investigators have confirmed this phenomenon on numerous occasions. Some visitors have felt a hand on their back while they stood in the room. There also have been reports of people being knocked to the floor and, in one case, even thrown across the room, by an invisible force. The latter scenario suggests the presence of a *poltergeist*, which draws its energy from the subconscious mind of a living person nearby.

The fifth floor is also home to the ghastly apparition of a young nurse. Back in the early 1930's, a floor nurse reported for duty one afternoon and, not finding anyone in the head nurse's office, decided to stay there. Because it was standard procedure to retrieve paperwork from the office when reporting for work, no one gave a second thought to her entering the office.

That evening, a worker from the cafeteria entered the office to collect empty dinner plates and silverware. Finding no dishes on the desk, he searched the cluttered room and noticed that the door leading to the small bathroom behind the office was ajar. Seeing no light coming from the bathroom, he gave the door a gentle push and turned the light on. There, he saw the young nurse's lifeless body hanging from the overhead pipes.

Local legend says she had been romantically involved with one of the doctors and had become pregnant. For years, visitors have seen her apparition floating in the doorway, likely guarding the room so others won't commit suicide there – or perhaps use it for other purposes. People have occasionally reported feeling a choking sensation when standing underneath the room's overhead pipes.

The building's fourth floor sees its share of ghostly activity as well. The most active area seems to be the old operating room, which is a consistent source of *orbs* – small concentrations of light – that appear in photos. Some investigators say the orbs are simply dust from the aging building, while others think they represent spiritual energy left behind by those who didn't survive the risky procedures performed there.

The most terrifying aspect of the operating room,

which is usually experienced just after daybreak, is the unmistakable aroma of cinnamon and other pastries baking in the sanatorium's kitchen. Located three stories below the operating room and a few paces to the north, the old kitchen's exhaust vents are still intact. There hasn't been electricity in the kitchen in many years.

As one might expect, some visitors speculate that cooks rise from the dead each morning and prepare breakfast for the ghosts who live at Waverly Hills. Others say the morning dew mixes with the steam residue that accumulated on the exhaust fans when they were in operation many years ago. The early morning aroma is frightening because it so clearly reminds us that Waverly Hills was a real place with real people, and those people are apparently still there.

Another consistent source of orbs is the facility's morgue, located on the first floor. Orbs of different sizes, shapes, and colors consistently appear in photos taken there. Drastic drops in temperature have also been reported in the morgue, despite the absence of electricity to power the old air conditioning and refrigeration units.

The absence of electricity seems to be a common thread among ghostly encounters in many parts of the building. On many occasions, visitors have seen lights burning in random patient rooms on different floors. Seen at random times throughout the night, the lights rarely burn longer than five minutes at a time. They always disappear before the guards reach the rooms to inspect them. The phenomenon usually occurs in one room at a time; however, there have been unconfirmed reports of entire sections of the building lighting up. Older witnesses have remarked that the glow emitted by the lights is reminiscent of the glow produced by gas-powered lights used in the 1930's.

If the glow of lights without electricity isn't strange

enough, the author and a friend had a frightening encounter that involved electrical wires sizzling. We were on the third floor investigating a corner room near one of the fire escapes when I suddenly began smelling the odor of wires burning. The odor was strongest near the doorway leading to the main hallway.

We cautiously stepped into the hallway. The odor seemed to be lingering there, and the dim glow of our flashlights was the only source of light. We shut off our flashlights and looked all around. Not seeing any kind of light, such as a fire or sparks, we turned on our flashlights and began looking for smoke. The odor had to be coming from somewhere.

We slowly made our way down the hall, checking each room and sniffing in different directions. The odor growing stronger as we walked, we kept walking until we reached the atrium, where the bitter odor was almost unbearable. Immediately, I heard the sizzling of two live wires touching each other. The source was very close. After 15 more minutes of sniffing and listening, we still had found nothing. By that time, the sound appeared to be coming from all different directions, yet no place in particular.

After changing our flashlight batteries, my friend pointed to some old-fashioned elevator doors and began telling me about the rooftop machinery used to raise and lower the elevator many years ago. The sizzling became louder as we approached the old elevator doors. To my shock and amazement, I discovered that the sound and the bitter odor – and now, the heat – were coming from an old button panel next to the elevator doors. There had been no electricity in that section of the building in a very long time.

It is hard to accept the notion that electricity with no known source can flow through old, crumpled wires and cause a short circuit. Reminding myself that former patients reportedly roam the halls of Waverly Hills, I reasoned that someone still living in the past, perhaps a patient, had been trying to use the elevator when we were there, in the present.

How can events that happened long ago still be seen happening, as if they are happening right now? Some researchers theorize that a *veil* exists between dimensions in time, and that the veil becomes thinner in certain places. This allows the events of one period to be experienced, to a limited degree, by those living in another period. Two separate groups of people could be living in the same building but at two different points in time. One group is living at a modern, state-of-the-art treatment facility, and the other group is investigating an old, abandoned tuberculosis hospital.

From photo orbs to recorded EVP, and from eighty-year-old pastries baking to a 1930's-era nurse protecting an office, the Waverly Hills Tuberculosis Sanatorium building is undoubtedly one of the most haunted locations in America. Despite the many different and often conflicting theories that attempt to explain the phenomena encountered there, most paranormal researchers will agree that many of its patients never left.

Despite all the ghostly activity reported in and around the old building, Waverly Hills Tuberculosis Sanatorium wasn't all about death and gloom. It was a place of caring, compassion, hope, and new beginnings, where a lucky few survived and went on to lead happy, productive lives. Many even returned to Waverly Hills and helped others combat the deadly disease. A handful of those who returned were husband-and-wife teams who had met for the first time when they, too, were patients there.

❧ THREE ❧

The Brown Mountain Lights

WITH THEIR DENSE PINE FORESTS, GUSHING STREAMS, and picturesque, fog-laden valleys, the Appalachian Mountains paint a timeless picture of nature. Standing atop a vista and gazing at the vast expanse of nature, one can't help but marvel at the beauty of the majestic Appalachians.

Come nightfall, however, the dense pine forests, flower-covered plateaus, and towering vistas fade into the darkness and come alive with the sounds of coyotes, mountain lions, hide-behinds, and other creatures of the night. The sound of a grunt in the distance, followed by the swishing of leaves behind you, awakens your senses and pumps your adrenaline. As you hurry back to your car, a tree branch crackles in the thicket ahead of you. What's there?

The Appalachian Mountains are enshrouded by an aura of mystery that has long been at the center of local lore. Tales of missing trappers, colossal creatures, and ghostly apparitions walking the forests are as much a part of Southern Appalachian culture as serpent handling, moonshine stills, and well-tuned banjos. Nearly every mountain has a bizarre tale to tell, but one mountain's claim to infamy goes well beyond the realm of traditional Appalachian lore.

Situated near Morganton, North Carolina, Brown Mountain has been home to mysterious ghost lights for centuries. The so-called *Brown Mountain Lights* have captured the attention of early Native Americans, explorers, the press, and even the U.S. government.

The lights flare at random locations along the side of the mountain and begin moving slowly through the trees. After a short time, they float upward to a point about 200 feet above the mountain's crest, and then pause. After pausing anywhere from one to seven minutes, the mysterious lights descend to the mountaintop and gradually fade away.

Although the lights usually follow a pattern, their behavior can be erratic at times. A single light will sometimes break up into several smaller lights, and then recombine to form another, much brighter light. At other times a light may appear, blink, and then vanish without floating upward.

The lights, which appear randomly, vary in color and brightness. They usually start out greenish-yellow and then transition into a whitish color. On several occasions, witnesses have reported seeing them turn reddish-orange. In terms of brightness, the lights usually start out dim and gradually become brighter as they rise above the mountain's crest, reaching their brightest point just before descending and fading away.

Few observers have tried to approach the lights because of the many boulders, dense thickets, and aggressive timber rattlers that separate the mountain from its main observation point, three-quarters of a mile away. The lights also have a short lifespan; they would most likely disappear before anyone reaches them from the observation point.

The Brown Mountain Lights appear more frequently during the fall, and they materialize under a wide variety of weather conditions. It is unknown why the lights appear more in the fall. The biggest mystery, however, is what the lights are, and why they only appear at Brown Mountain as opposed to the other mountains nearby.

According to Native American legend, the lights date back to the year 1200 A.D. when an intense battle broke out between the Cherokee and Catawba tribes. The battle lasted an entire day and claimed the lives of many warriors. In the bloody aftermath, maidens lit torches and spent the entire night combing Brown Mountain for their fallen warriors. Now, centuries later, the tragic scene replays itself in the form of a residual haunting. The Brown Mountain Lights are allegedly the torches being carried by the maidens.

Another legend, made popular in the bluegrass song called *Brown Mountain Light*, states that the mountain got its name from a nineteenth century plantation owner who became lost while hunting on the mountain. When the man failed to return, his slaves took lanterns and searched the mountain for him. They, too, were lost. The Brown Mountain Lights are allegedly their lanterns.

Many legends attempt to explain the Brown Mountain Lights, but the two mentioned above seem to be the most popular. There are also tales of UFO's, fairies, gnomes, and other entities making the eerie lights appear. The scientific community also has attempted to explain the phenomenon.

In 1771, German engineer Geraud Will de Brahm explored the region and heard unfamiliar sounds near Brown Mountain. He wrote in his journal that the sounds most likely came from airborne nitrous vapors combusting simultaneously. Although he made no mention of having seen the mysterious lights, it makes sense that the combustion of nitrous vapor would produce light. However, de Brahm never stated what caused the vapor to evolve and ignite in the first place and, more importantly, why the phenomenon is confined to Brown Mountain. Other mountains in the region are almost identical to Brown Mountain in many regards.

Years later, the United States government became interested in the Brown Mountain Lights. The phenomenon was investigated once by the U.S. Weather Service, once by the Smithsonian Institution, and twice by the U.S. Geological Survey.

The Geological Survey's first investigation, conducted in 1913, concluded that the lights were reflections of locomotive lights in the Catawba Valley. However, three years later, severe flooding in the area knocked out railroad bridges and suspended train travel for weeks. The phantom lights continued to appear. The Geological Survey's second investigation concluded that the lights come from the spontaneous combustion of marsh gas (methane). Their report met with considerable skepticism due to the area's lack of marshes, dried ponds, and other methane sources.

The U.S. Weather Service investigated the Brown Mountain Lights in 1941 and concluded that they are similar to the Andes Lights in South America. While their observation may be true, it doesn't shed much light on the mystery. Suggesting that the lights aren't unique doesn't adequately explain their origin.

The most notable scientific investigation of the Brown Mountain Lights occurred between the 1970's and 1980's when a team of scientists from the U.S. Department of Defense's Oak Ridge National Laboratory studied the lights. The team, called ORION (Oak Ridge Isochronous Observation Network), worked in conjunction with a group called *The Enigma Project.*

The joint group proved that reflected light could in fact produce balls of light above the crest of Brown Mountain. They also noted that the Brown Mountain Lights had been observed long before electricity, trains, and automobiles came to the area. In another test, they unsuccessfully tried to reproduce the lights through seismic activity.

Despite all the time, money, and effort spent on researching the mysterious lights, an adequate explanation of their origin has yet to evolve. Until that happens, the Brown Mountain Lights will remain one of Appalachia's biggest and most bizarre mysteries.

❧ FOUR ❧

The Devil's Tramping Ground

NESTLED AMONG TOWERING OAKS AND WHISPERING pines in a forest near Siler City, North Carolina, is a barren circle of land that has baffled researchers and curiosity-seekers alike for more than a century.

Known as *The Devil's Tramping Ground*, the near-perfect circle measures about 21 feet in diameter and shows no sign of plant life other than scant patches of weeds. Despite the abundance of plants growing just outside the circle, attempts to grow plants within the circle have been futile. One researcher claims that a live flower he planted inside the circle died within 24 hours.

The absence of plant life in the circle is but a small part of the mystery surrounding The Devil's Tramping Ground. On many occasions, visitors to the area were shocked to learn that their pets were afraid of venturing into the circle.

In one case, a man led his dog toward the circle and, when they reached the edge, the dog spooked and began

tugging in the opposite direction, eventually snapping its leash in half. The dog, terrified, scampered back to the man's car. In another case, a family reported that their usually well-behaved dog began running back and forth around the circle's edge, barking and growling at something in the circle. The family saw nothing in the circle.

Most people would feel inclined to dismiss these accounts as being situations in which pets became uncomfortable in strange surroundings; however, even the undisputed kings and queens of the forest – the wild animals who native to the area – shun the mysterious circle. Hunters have seen wild animals walk up to the circle's edge, look into the circle, and then walk around its edge to reach the other side.

On one occasion, a man hunting nearby shot and wounded a deer. The deer lay on the ground motionless for a short time, then suddenly jumped up and scurried away. The hunter followed the wounded deer all the way to the circle's edge, where it suddenly stopped and changed direction, avoiding the circle. The deer resumed its original course after bypassing the circle.

This incident brings to mind an important question: Why would a wounded deer, when fleeing a hunter brandishing a high-powered rifle, risk almost certain death by slowing down to bypass the circle? Perhaps the deer sensed more danger inside the circle than in the woods directly behind him. Whatever its reason was for avoiding the mysterious circle, the deer apparently used good judgment, for it ultimately escaped.

The outcome might have been different had the deer gone into the circle. The following picture, taken inside the circle, shows a wild animal's badly mangled carcass. There are no visible clues as to what caused the animal's death. The ground matter is composed of leaves and pine needles from nearby trees, as well as chunks of the

animal's white fur and a set of hooves.

The circle's negative appeal isn't limited to plants and animals. Radios and cell phones often experience reception problems inside the circle but work fine outside the circle. There have also been reports of brand new batteries not working inside the circle but mysteriously coming to life when taken outside the circle. Propane stoves and coal oil lanterns have been known to burn out prematurely when placed inside the circle.

Wilmington Morning Star reporter H.T. Ivy gave the mysterious circle its name in his 1882 article entitled, "The Devil's Tramping Ground." The first commercially published account of the phenomenon, Ivy's article paved the way for at least 25 newspaper articles, 15 books, and countless magazine articles to be written about the mysterious circle.

Some legends about The Devil's Tramping Ground date back to the early 1800's when Native Americans and early white settlers lived in the area. The most popular legend says the Devil visits the site nightly and paces in a circle as he plans evil deeds for the next day. His extreme heat allegedly keeps the ground sterile.

A Native American legend states that an evil tribal chief was murdered in cold blood at what is now the center of the circle. His blood poisoned the ground where he fell, thereby cursing it forever. Another legend states that a Native American boy was hunting in the forest one day and happened upon a snake, which bit him, and he died on the spot. Those who found him performed a sacred ritual at the site, asking the spirits to ensure that no grass or animal ever be allowed there.

Others have concluded that extraterrestrial beings are responsible for the many anomalies associated with the circle. Some believe that a UFO landed on the spot and made the ground regress to a period in which there was little plant life in the area. Others believe the circle was the point of impact when a meteorite plummeted to earth long ago, and that space matter tainted the soil.

In addition to legends about the Devil pacing the circle, Native Americans placing a curse on it, and extraterrestrials landing on it, a few scientific theories have been offered up.

One theory states that the soil never regained its fertility after an old barn was razed. However, historians insist that there was never a structure on the site. A similar theory states that grain residue from a once-present silo over-fertilized the ground beneath it, which sterilized the soil and created the nearly perfect barren circle. Although this theory seems logically sound, there has never been a structure on the site.

Another, somewhat humorous theory suggests that the site was once home to a mule that was chained to a post and forced to walk in circles to power a grinder. His continuous walking caused the ground beneath his feet to become worn and sterile.

Many years ago, the North Carolina Department of Agriculture tested soil samples taken from inside the circle and found high levels of sodium. While this may raise an eyebrow, it falls short of explaining why animals shun the circle and why radios and cell phones often lose their signal inside the circle.

An independent scientist recently visited the site and conducted a series of tests on the soil. He gathered samples from inside the circle, from the ring around it, and from an area just outside the circle. He tested each sample and found nothing out of the ordinary. As a final test, he placed each soil sample in a different cup and planted something in each cup. Plants grew from the samples taken inside and outside the circle, but nothing grew in the sample taken from its ring.

The Devil's Tramping Ground remains a mystery. No adequate explanation exists as to why the ground inside

GHOSTLY CRIES FROM DIXIE ❖

the circle is sterile, why animals avoid the circle, and why radios and cell phones have trouble picking up a signal inside the circle.

While some might consider the phenomenon an urban legend of sorts, it is quite real to those who encounter it. Whether it's a natural force, a Native American curse, ET and his friends from outer space, or even Old Lucifer himself, no one knows. Something very old and powerful is there. Be careful.

❧ FIVE ❧

The Headless Conductor at Chapel Hill

ITUATED AMONG THE ROLLING HILLS AND IMMACULATE farmlands of Middle Tennessee, the quaint little town of Chapel Hill boasts a church, a school, a cafe, and a residential section that's characterized by Mayberry-like sidewalks and immaculate old homes surrounded by white picket fences.

Chapel Hill sprang into existence in the late 1800's when the Louisville and Nashville Railroad was built through the area. The town became a stop on the railroad's Nashville-to-Birmingham segment, hosting a steady stream of passenger and freight trains each day. In later years, the advent of interstates and commercial air travel made rail travel obsolete; railroading's golden age had come to an end. Today, only an occasional freight train roars through Chapel Hill.

A town like Chapel Hill, reminiscent of *Main Street, USA*, isn't where one would expect to encounter the supernatural. However, a tragic event that happened on the outskirts of town nearly seventy years ago triggered a haunting that frightens tourists and locals alike.

The story begins on a winter night back in the 1930's when trains 1 and 2 were scheduled to pass each other at a siding just north of town. When train 1 was about five minutes away, train 2's conductor switched his train onto the siding and began waiting for the other train to pass. Once the other train had passed, he would switch his train back onto the main track and have the engineer proceed.

Five minutes later, train 1, its headlight shining brightly and its whistle crooning loudly, rounded a sharp curve and came into view. In less than a minute, it was roaring past train 2. The intense vibrations made the conductor lose his footing in the loose gravel between the tracks. A fraction of a second later, a dull, clunking sound, similar to that of a watermelon being chopped open, came from the rails beneath train 1.

Train 2's engineer patiently awaited his conductor's lantern signal indicating that they could proceed. He looked out both sides of the locomotive cab and saw nothing but the rear of train 1 off in the distance. Everything else was dark and still; there were no lights, no sounds, nothing.

After fifteen minutes without receiving an "all clear" signal, the engineer, his train now running late, decided to look for the conductor. Stepping down from the locomotive and walking the entire length of his train, he saw no sign of the conductor, not even his lantern or the faint glow of a cigarette. He shouted the conductor's name several times but there was no answer. A minute later, he shouted the conductor's name again, and still nothing.

Worried and frustrated, the engineer turned around and began walking back to the locomotive. After walking a short distance, he spotted the conductor's broken lantern lying on the ground near the main track. Then he noticed a small cloud of mist rising from the main track near the lantern. He thought the mist was coming from a smoldering cigarette butt or possibly an ember that had fallen from train 1's locomotive as it rumbled by. Nevertheless, where was the conductor? As he leaned over to pick up the broken lantern, he paused briefly and glanced up the main track.

The conductor's severed head, partially crushed and facing upward, lay next to a blood-spattered rail barely six feet away. A small cloud of mist hovered above the open cut as the conductor's remaining body heat escaped into the cold night air. The rest of his body lay a few feet away.

The engineer ran a quarter mile up the track, to the nearest crossing, and flagged down a motorist. Sherriff's deputies and medical personnel reached the scene thirty minutes later. They found the conductor's body where the engineer had said it was, but they couldn't find his head. To this day, no one knows what happened to the conductor's head. Some feel that wild animals detected the scent of fresh blood and dragged it away; others think it became lodged underneath a passing train.

The siding where the tragedy occurred is long gone; a road now crosses the single track that runs through the site. Woods, marshes, and a few modest homes dot the rural landscape nearby. At night, an eerie silence befalls the area. A hound dog occasionally yelps and howls in the distance; an occasional car or truck can be heard off in the distance, and the lonely crossing gate's bell rings when a train roars by.

Although the area seems peaceful at first glance, a headless figure carrying a lantern and walking down the track late at night has frightened residents and tourists alike for years. The ghastly figure wanders up and down a half-mile stretch of track, sometimes for an hour or longer, before fading away. The figure is oblivious to onlookers unless they throw rocks or try to take pictures, in which case it suddenly vanishes.

The figure occasionally walks past onlookers standing only fifty feet away. One such group was a Nashville television crew who captured the phenomenon on film. As one might imagine, the segment drew a great deal of skepticism when it aired. Several other witnesses, who weren't related to the TV crew, were on hand when the filming took place. They later said that the TV crew never staged the incident.

The phenomenon isn't always a male figure confined to the railroad track. It sometimes manifests in the form of a small, flickering light at the edge of the nearby woods. Many believe that someone is playing pranks in the woods because the sound of footsteps often accompanies the apparition. However, for years, people have searched the woods for the culprit and found nothing. In some cases, the figure started out walking on the railroad track and ventured into the woods a short time later.

On one occasion, three onlookers decided to pursue the figure after seeing it walk into the woods. As they neared the woods, someone – or something – began pelting them with rocks. Sore and bruised, the sleuths returned two days later and found a stockpile of hand-size rocks and old railroad spikes just inside the woods. Their finding suggests that people sometimes hide in the woods and throw rocks at onlookers; however, leaves and vines covered the pile of rocks in such a way that no one could have touched it without disturbing the soggy leaves.

The figure appears sporadically, usually between the hours of 12:30 and 2:00 A.M. No one knows why the figure chooses to walk during those hours; some researchers have speculated that the conductor died within that timeframe. Validating such a hunch would be tricky, however, because decapitation is an instant type of death; it doesn't take a person's heart ninety minutes to stop beating after a train's wheel slices their head off.

The headless apparition isn't the only phenomena experienced along the railroad track in Chapel Hill; the site produces its share of anomalous pictures as well. Human-shaped concentrations of mist, showers of multi-colored orbs, and stretches of ectoplasm zigzagging across the track have mysteriously appeared in photos and videos made at the site.

In the year 2000, a Nashville author and investigator visited the site and shot close-up footage of an orb changing size and color. The video first showed a large gray orb moving from side to side as it floated up the railroad track and away from the camera. After about thirty seconds, it turned yellowish and became larger. The orb continued getting larger as it floated up the track, finally turning orange and fading away after about three minutes.

There have been few attempts to explain the phenomena along the railroad track in Chapel Hill. Local opinion ranges from complete skepticism to absolute certainty. While some locals insist the accident never happened, others say their grandparents knew the engineer and conductor, and that the accident did in fact happen. Non-locals have theorized that a rock wall located a mile north of the site creates the phenomena by reflecting the headlights of oncoming trains. If that's the case, then why do people experience the phenomena on nights when no trains pass through the area?

We will most likely never discover the true origin of the headless figure that walks the railroad track and haunts the woods near Chapel Hill, Tennessee. He continues to frighten residents and tourists, and he is very real in the minds of those who see him. Watch him;

take pictures of him; yell at him; but whatever you do, don't follow him into the woods.

❧ SIX ❧

Mary at the Orpheum

A DISCUSSION OF MEMPHIS GHOSTS WOULDN'T BE complete without mention of Elvis Presley, whose spiritual likeness reportedly roams Graceland and half a dozen other locations in the Bluff City. Within hours of his passing, reports of "Elvis sightings" began coming in from every part of the world, from Memphis, Tennessee to Memphis, Egypt. In no time, paranormal researchers began converging on Memphis in record numbers to pursue the elusive ghost of Elvis Presley.

In a matter of months, tabloid newspapers turned The King's legacy into a scandal. The many "Elvis sightings" reported by the tabloids were mere hoaxes and not worthy of serious investigation. Non-local researchers went home, and local researchers began investigating the ghost of a little girl who has been haunting the Orpheum Theatre for the past 81 years.

Built in 1928 and located a block from the world-famous Beale Street Entertainment District, the Orpheum Theatre has been at the center of Memphis' fine-arts community for eighty-one years, hosting the likes of George Burns, Cary Grant, and Sammy Davis,

Jr. along the way. The Orpheum's success continues today with frequent black-tie events that draw legions of dedicated patrons from across the region.

In its early years, the Orpheum presented children's matinees on Saturday and Sunday afternoons. Mary, whose family spent most weekends shopping on South Main Street, was one of the many children who flocked to the Orpheum each weekend to catch a matinee. For her parents, letting her watch a matinee was more affordable than buying her everything she wanted from each shop she visited.

Mary loved the matinees and the brief time she spent away from her parents each weekend. Each week, she counted down the days until she would be riding the trolley from the train station to the Orpheum. If she had been good all week, her parents would take her to a doll shop after the matinee. Mary was always on her best behavior, for she loved dolls and she loved seeing the matinees.

The late fall of 1928 brought the highly acclaimed Broadway musical, *Sunny Days*, to the brand new Orpheum Theatre. Mary was excited to learn that a children's matinee would be performed on the final weekend of the production's two-week run. Her aunt had already seen the play and told her many good things about it. The next two weeks seemed like eternity, but the magic day arrived before she knew it. Waking up earlier than usual that morning, Mary and her parents ate breakfast at a local café before catching the train that ran twice daily between Memphis and their hometown of Byhalia, Mississippi.

After the 45-minute train ride, Mary and her parents stood in line outside the Orpheum and waited for the doors to open. After a few minutes, Mary grew impatient and walked across the street to look at dolls in store windows. Her parents agreed to keep her place in the line, provided she didn't venture too far away.

Mary walked up to the first store window and spotted the most beautiful doll she had seen in a long time. She knew her parents would buy it for her because she had been good that week, but there was little chance of it still being there after the matinee. Other girls were already eyeing the pretty doll and begging their parents to buy it for them. Mary decided to make a mad dash across the street and get the money from her parents. A fast-approaching trolley didn't faze her; she would simply outrun it.

While sprinting across the street, Mary's foot snagged the trolley track and sent her crashing onto the pavement. Hurt and somewhat dazed, she glanced in the direction of the trolley. It was only ten feet away. She was so scared that she couldn't move. She lay between the rails helplessly, trembling and crying as the trolley came closer. The trolley operator engaged the emergency brake, but it was too late; the trolley was moving fast and Mary was too close. Seconds later, the trolley hit her.

Despite having been hit by a trolley going fifteen miles per hour, Mary was still alive and in desperate need of medical attention. Her parents and several onlookers rushed to her side and gently picked her up. They carried her into the theatre, which had just opened its doors. The lobby was too crowded for Mary to receive proper medical attention, so her parents carried her into the auditorium and placed her in a seat where she could rest comfortably until a doctor arrived. It was too late. She lost consciousness and died five minutes later.

Not long after that tragic day, theatre workers and moviegoers began seeing the apparition of a young girl sitting in seat C-5, the seat in which Mary died. Although she doesn't appear frequently, Mary has appeared consistently over the years, always wearing a 1920's-period dress and gazing at the stage. She appears almost human to some witnesses, while others say she looks more like a doll or wax figure. Everyone agrees that the apparition is Mary.

She doesn't confine herself to seat C-5. People have seen her standing in the lobby, walking the hallways in the basement, and sitting in different parts of the auditorium. She reportedly loves the upper balconies. Surprisingly, Mary's appearances don't usually coincide with movies, plays, or similar events. Cleaning crews have seen her when the theatre was closed; actors have seen her when they were rehearsing, and moviegoers occasionally see her sitting in the seat behind them. Mary can appear anywhere, and at any time.

Some feel that Mary also haunts the old trolley track that still runs past the Orpheum. Child-like cries are sometimes heard coming from the track, even when no children are around. There is no known connection between the phantom cries and Mary's tragedy, but it's possible that a residual haunting is taking place.

Mary's only chance to see *Sunny Days* at the Orpheum was thwarted by tragedy. For the past 81 years, she has been waiting patiently for the play to begin. She will likely stay there because the play hasn't been performed anywhere in over 75 years. If a modern theatre company were to resurrect *Sunny Days* and perform it at the Orpheum, Mary would most likely *cross over* and leave the place.

❧ SEVEN ❧

The Bell Witch

ETWEEN 1817 AND 1821, A MALEVOLENT ENTITY tormented the John Bell family and held middle Tennessee's Red River community in its sinister grasp. The entity made noises; it tortured small children; it predicted the future; it knew the Bible, and it allegedly killed a man. What was it? What was its purpose? Today, almost 200 years later, the mystery remains unsolved.

The story begins in the winter of 1805 when John and Lucy Bell moved their family from North Carolina to the Red River Settlement in middle Tennessee. Their first twelve years at Red River brought 3 more children, 100 more acres of farmland, and John Bell's appointment as an elder of Red River Baptist Church. Although their first twelve years in Tennessee had gone well, the Bell family's luck would soon run out. What John Bell experienced on a chilly fall morning in 1817 signaled the beginning of what would change his life and the lives of his family forever.

On that fateful morning, Bell was hunting in a cornfield near his orchard when he happened upon an animal that was unlike anything he had ever seen. It had the body of a dog and the head of a rabbit. Standing in a small clearing about twenty feet away, the creature gazed at Bell intently with its beady red eyes. Bell, an excellent marksman, fired several shots at the animal. It didn't flinch; it sat completely still. Bell fired another shot and, without so much as a yelp, the mysterious creature vanished right in front of him. Thinking the animal had been a mix-bred dog, Bell tried to forget about the incident and continue hunting, although he knew he had hit the animal between its eyes at least twice.

As winter set in and the nights grew colder, Bell and his family began hearing raps on the outside walls of their log house each night. Bell and his sons would rush outside to see who was there, but they never found a culprit. The slaves were always asleep in their quarters; Old Caesar was always asleep on the front porch, and the horses never appeared spooked. The mysterious raps grew louder and more frequent with each night that passed.

The younger Bell children soon began waking up at night, complaining of rats gnawing at their bedposts and chains being dragged across the floor. John and Lucy Bell would rush to the children's bedroom and comfort them while the older children, John, Jr. and Drewry, searched for the seemingly invisible culprit. A few weeks later, something began tugging at the children's sheets and pillowcases when they tried to fall asleep each night. The tugging would continue until John and Lucy Bell rushed into the bedroom. When they left, it would resume.

The children became brave one night and decided to resist the tugs with all their might. Just as they had expected, the tugging began about ten minutes after they went to bed. Daughter Betsy, who was then eleven years old, whispered to her siblings, "one…, two…, three…." Holding their sheets tightly, the children tugged in the opposite direction as hard as they could. Instantly, they felt a cold, hard slap across their faces, a slap so loud and forceful that it awakened everyone in the house. When the rest of the family rushed in to investigate, they found the children's teary faces covered with welts. As was the case with the raps on the outside walls and the sounds of rats and chains coming from the floor, a culprit was never found.

The mysterious force – whatever it was – tormented Betsy Bell the most. Every night, the force would pull her hair, slap her, and physically beat her, even when her parents and siblings were in the room with her. The red handprints on Betsy's face were nothing compared to the black, blue, and yellowish bruises that often covered her body. Betsy Bell lived in fear. Her friends at school began to question why she always appeared sleepy and why her arms were always covered with bruises. She told them nothing because her father, fearing negative repercussions from the church, had ordered his family to keep the matter a secret.

The entity soon moved outside the house. On rainy nights, the Bells often saw candles flickering in the distant fields and heard an unusual humming sound in the wind. These phenomena, along with the strange raps on the wall and the brutal abuse experienced by the children, was enough to convince John and Lucy Bell that their family was living at the mercy of a powerful entity with a mind and a will all its own.

The first break in the case came in the spring of 1818 when the family began hearing faint, whistling sounds in response to the questions they asked the entity. The whistles eventually grew into whispers. Jumbled and difficult to hear at first, the whispers sounded like an old woman crying or trying to hum a church hymn. Over a six-month period, the faint whispers evolved into a loud, clear, and unmistakable voice. When the entity was content, it spoke in a low tone similar to notes being played on a cello; when angry, it spoke in a shrill tone.

Despite the entity's intelligence and newfound ability to speak, family members were unsuccessful in making it discuss its origin and purpose. After more than a year of terror, torment, and abuse of his family by the sinister entity, John Bell decided to seek the help of his closest friend and neighbor, James Johnston. This would be the first time a Bell family member discussed the entity with an outside person.

Puzzled by Bell's story, Johnston agreed to spend the night with the Bells and try to experience the entity himself. Johnston came and ate dinner, sang some hymns, and led a prayer before everyone retired for the evening. Not long after he went to bed, Johnston began hearing strange noises. Their location and intensity suggested that the entity was aware of his presence. A terrified James Johnston sprang from his bed and exclaimed, "In the name of the Lord, who are you and why are you here!" Johnston's outburst silenced the entity for the rest of the night.

At breakfast, Johnston told John Bell that the entity was a sprit and that members of the clergy should be made aware of it. Bell agreed, and the two men went to visit the three local preachers. Two days later, every fencepost near the Bell home had a horse tied to it, and curiosity-seekers filled the front yard. Some even accused the Bells of fabricating a hoax in order to make money, although they never charged anyone a cent. The entity's demonstrations weren't limited to the Bells and Mr. Johnston; anyone who visited the Bell home could experience the demonstrations.

News of a supernatural entity taking up residence in John Bell's home spread like wildfire. Before too long, the Red River Baptist Church excommunicated Bell for allegedly charging a man too much interest on the sale of a slave. By the summer of 1818, the entity had reached the point where it could assume different personalities and speak in different voices. It liked to sing hymns, quote the Bible, and intelligently debate issues of the day. By 1819, the entity was no longer confined to the Bell farm. It attended social gatherings throughout the community, where it would gab like the town gossip, yell like the town drunk, sing like an angel, and curse like a sailor.

The entity took great pleasure in keeping people on their best behavior. If Joe Edwards missed church because he had been drunk the night before, the entire congregation would hear about it. If a kid went fishing instead of going to school, the entire school – and the kid's parents – would hear about it. If someone missed church for a legitimate reason, as Lucy Bell once did, the entity would visit the person and repeat the sermon for them.

Mrs. Bell missed church one Sunday morning in the summer of 1819. Concerned about her health, two preachers visited the Bell home that evening to say a prayer for her. As the prayer was being said, the entity chimed in and quoted both preachers' sermons, word for word, and using their actual voices. Both sermons had been preached at 11 o'clock that morning at churches that were thirteen miles apart.

The entity also took pleasure in checking on people's whereabouts. Jesse Bell, the oldest son, had moved away from home by 1819 and was living nearby. One summer day, Jesse had occasion to visit Kentucky on business. He ended up staying longer than he had planned. Having not seen her son in three days, Lucy Bell asked the entity to check on him. It responded, "Wait a minute, Luce; I will go and see for you!" It returned a minute later, proclaiming that Jesse had returned home and was reading a book. Jesse visited his parents' home the next morning and confirmed the entity's revelation, saying that his front door had opened and closed by itself the night before.

Although the entity liked to mind people's business, quote sermons, and abuse the Bell family, it went to great lengths in hiding its identity and purpose. It never gave a consistent or credible answer to perhaps the most important question of all: Who are you, and why are you here? It once answered, "I am a spirit. I was once very happy, but my bones have been disturbed." On another occasion, it claimed to have buried a trunk full of money nearby. It also claimed to be the spirit of a child buried in North Carolina.

Reverend James Gunn, fed up with the entity's unwillingness to reveal its identity, phrased the

important question in such a way that a truthful answer couldn't be avoided – or so he thought. The entity replied, "I can not lie. I am old Cate Batts' witch, and I am here to torment ol' Jack Bell out of his life!" "Ol' Jack Bell" was the nickname given John Bell by the entity. The entity's revelation shocked people; John Bell was a well-respected member of the Red River Settlement, and there was no known reason why someone, or something, would want him dead.

The entity's self-proclaimed identity didn't shock people, however. A large and rather eccentric woman, Cate Batts had always been at the center of gossip and controversy. People also took an instant disliking to her because she wasn't in the best of financial conditions. Some even thought she dabbled in the occult because of her uncanny ability to achieve personal gain from the misfortunes of others. Others thought it odd that she collected a brass pin from every woman she met; the pin, they believed, would give her power over the person who gave it to her. She is rumored to have stuck each pin into a large stump near her home.

Well aware of the entity's antics and demonstrations, Mrs. Batts became furious upon learning that she was the prime suspect. She visited everyone in the community and told them she had nothing to do with the entity or the disturbances in John Bell's home. Although modern research has since cleared Mrs. Batts' name in connection with the disturbances, many still mistakenly believe that she was the culprit. After the entity's revelation, people began calling it *Kate*, a name to which it would answer from that point on.

A short time later, *Kate* introduced four new and distinct characters that she called her "Witch Family." The first character, "Blackdog," spoke in a raspy, feminine tone and was the self-proclaimed leader of the Witch Family. The characters named "Mathematics" and "Cypocryphy" sounded like little girls. The fourth character, "Jerusalem," sounded like a little boy. Every night for nearly a month, the drunken Witch Family visited the Bell home and sang hymns, shouted profanities at each other, and saturated the house with the smell of whiskey. "Blackdog" repeatedly cursed and chastised the other characters during the nightly demonstrations, which usually lasted two hours.

Although the Witch Family usually manifested as a disembodied chorus of unique and often profane voices, a woman and three children, believed to be the Witch Family, were spotted in a field one morning in the early fall of 1819. The apparition occurred at the farm of Esther Porter. Esther, the oldest daughter of John and Lucy Bell, lived with her husband on a farm near Sturgeon Creek, not far from the Bell home.

As Esther collected eggs one morning, she noticed a woman and three children – a little boy and two little girls – standing in a field across the road from her. When she yelled to them, they ignored her and walked to the edge of the woods. They located four saplings and bent then at a 90-degree angle, then began bouncing up and down on them. Esther had originally thought the people were new neighbors, but as she kept watching, she began to realize that something wasn't right about them. It was the middle of summer, yet they were pale; she had said hello to them, but they didn't respond. Perhaps most frightening of all, their eyes had been fixated on her the entire time.

When Esther's husband Alex returned later that morning, she tried to point out the mysterious figures. He couldn't see them; all he saw were the bent saplings bouncing up and down. As soon as Esther handed him his gun, the figures leapt off the saplings and took cover behind an old log. The little boy peeked over a knot in the log, and then ducked behind it again. Ten seconds later, the boy's head popped up from behind the log once again. He immediately ducked back down. At Esther's insistence, Alex took aim at the knot and blew it to pieces. Ten minutes later, the strange figures still had not emerged from behind the log. Esther and Alex walked across the road and learned that the figures had vanished.

That evening, *Kate* visited John Bell's house and told everyone about how Alex Porter had broke "Jerusalem's" arm from seventy-five yards away. Porter's excellent marksmanship was apparently all it took to scare the Witch Family away, for they never appeared again.

Although *Kate* belittled and physically abused most of John Bell's family, she seemed quite fond of Lucy Bell. In the winter of 1819, Mrs. Bell became ill with pleurisy and took to her bed. It wasn't long before she lost her appetite and strength. A worried *Kate* continually asked her if she was okay. One afternoon, grapes and hazelnuts began falling from the ceiling; they landed in the bed next to Mrs. Bell's hand. She thanked *Kate* for the grapes and nuts, but she didn't eat them.

"What is wrong, Luce? Why aren't you eating?" Kate asked.

"I'm sorry, Kate, but my hands aren't strong enough to crack the nuts open."

"Oh, but Luce, I will help you crack them!"

The nuts suddenly began cracking open by themselves, and Mrs. Bell ate them.

Aside from Mrs. Bell, the only people *Kate* seemed to treat nicely were those who paid her a lot of attention. The more attention she received, the stronger she became. Skeptics, on the other hand, usually fell out of *Kate's* good graces very quickly and often experienced ridicule and physical abuse.

Perhaps the best-known skeptic to visit the Bell home was Major General Andrew Jackson, who lived in nearby Nashville but owned land close to the Red River Settlement. The Bells' three oldest sons had fought under Jackson in the War of 1812. Although Jackson had heard of *Kate*, it wasn't until late 1819 that he realized the case involved three of his former soldiers. A curious yet skeptical Jackson decided to visit *Kate*.

As Jackson's entourage approached the Bell property line, the horses spooked and the wagons suddenly came to a halt. Jackson and his men yelled and cursed at the horses, and even tried pushing them, but their efforts were useless. Jackson then heard whispering sounds coming from the trees along the lane.

"Boys, that whispering must be that old 'Bell Witch' we've been hearing about!" Jackson exclaimed.

"That's all for now, gentlemen," said a disembodied voice.

"What do you mean, 'for now'?" Jackson retorted.

"You're just a bunch of old frauds," the voice

proclaimed, "and I'll see you again this evening!"

The horses then started moving.

That evening in the Bell home, a man in Jackson's entourage removed his pistol, loaded it with a shiny silver bullet, and told everyone he was a world-famous "witch killer." Jackson laughed hysterically. The man went on and on, bragging that *Kate* was aware of his presence and was afraid to try anything.

Suddenly, an invisible force slapped the man across his face, kicked his posterior region, and pulled him out the front door by the tip of his nose. *Kate* then spoke up and told Jackson there was yet another fraud in his entourage, and that she would expose him the following night. Despite his entourage's desperate pleas to leave, Jackson insisted on staying at the Bell home to find out who the other fraud was.

In a strange turn of events, Andrew Jackson and his entourage left before daybreak and never returned. What made Jackson change his mind remains a mystery to this day. Jackson, after becoming President of the United States, allegedly said, "I'd rather fight the entire British Army than deal with the old Bell Witch!"

In the weeks following Jackson's visit, *Kate* began to focus more on the mission she had originally set out to accomplish, which was to torment John Bell to his grave. She continued to profess her strong dislike for him, often slapping him across his face and reiterating her vow to kill him. No one understood why she wanted him dead; she never stated her reasons.

For some time, John Bell had suffered from a mysterious illness that caused his tongue to swell and his face to go numb. As the condition worsened, he grew weaker and began experiencing violent seizures; he also found it difficult to maintain the coordination in his feet. Over time, it became painfully obvious that *Kate* had been serious when she said she wanted Mr. Bell to suffer; she had been the evil force behind all of Mr. Bell's health problems.

One morning in the fall of 1820, John Bell and his son Richard set out to visit the hog pen and separate the hogs. Every few feet they walked, *Kate* either knocked Mr. Bell to the ground or ripped his shoes from his feet.

Bell became depressed after the hog pen incident. He had been suffering from ill health for a long time; he had trouble walking; and most importantly, he was being abused physically and ridiculed verbally by someone, or something, he couldn't even see. *Kate* often reminded his family, friends, and neighbors about her plan to make him suffer until his very last breath.

John Bell's health continued to decline over the fall and early winter. December found him confined to his bed permanently, with *Kate* at his bedside cursing him, slapping him, and spitting on him. John Bell died on the morning of December 20, 1820. He was 70.

Immediately after Bell's death, his family and friends noticed a strange, dark liquid in a medicine vial next to his bed. The vial had contained a clear liquid when Bell's doctor had delivered it the day before. John Bell, Jr. turned the vial upside down and let a drop of the odorous liquid fall onto the family cat's tongue. The cat immediately jumped three feet into the air, rolled halfway over, and landed on the floor. It died instantly.

The doctor soon arrived at the Bell home and sniffed the medicine vial. Unable to identify the odor, he offered to take the vial with him and analyze its contents. Before anyone could say anything, Professor Richard Powell jerked the vial away from the doctor and threw it into the fireplace. It exploded into a bright blue flame, and then shot up the chimney.

Powell, a well-educated man from North Carolina, was the Red River community's schoolmaster. Having taught several of the Bell children, he was good friends with the family. Powell often expressed his fondness for Betsy Bell, who happened to be his student at the time. He never gave a reason as to why he threw the medicine vial into the fire.

John Bell's funeral was one of the largest funerals ever held in Robertson County, Tennessee. Three preachers eulogized him, and the service lasted nearly two hours. *Kate* laughed and cheered as the large crowd of mourners walked away from the Bell family cemetery. She didn't stop until the very last mourner had left.

The winter of 1820-21 was especially hard on the Bells; the gloomy days and bitterly cold nights dragged on forever, it seemed. Life was different without John Bell around to fend for his family and run his farm, but everyone knew he had moved on to a better place. The only sign of Kate's presence was an occasional whisper or a lone knock on the wall. This was very different from the cursing, ghastly apparitions, and brutal beatings that the Bells had been forced to endure over the past four years. It seemed as if *Kate* had accomplished her mission and would be leaving soon; however, she had another matter to handle, and this time it involved Betsy Bell.

Over the past year, Betsy had become romantically involved with Joshua Gardner, a young man who lived nearby. Their courtship involved long walks and lazy picnics along the Red River, socializing at school and church functions, and visiting each other's families on occasion. *Kate* had very little to say about their courtship, but she became furious upon learning of their engagement.

Day and night, she screamed into Betsy's ear repeatedly, "Please, Betsy Bell, don't marry Joshua Gardner!" When asked why she was opposed to Betsy and Joshua's engagement, *Kate* would only say that Betsy would never be happy with Joshua; no other reason was ever given. Despite being harassed constantly, Betsy and Joshua agreed to stand strong and not allow *Kate* to ruin their plans for a life together. They loved each other very much; their parents were supportive, and their friends wished them the best.

The lovers endured much torment over the next two months. Betsy experienced episodes similar to those she had experienced in the past when *Kate* would slap her face, tie her hair in knots, and beat her severely. Over time, *Kate's* incessant screaming and violent physical attacks against Betsy took a toll on the engagement.

On Easter Monday of 1821, Betsy, Joshua, and some friends went down to the Red River for a picnic. After eating, Betsy and Joshua went fishing together at the mouth of a nearby spring. Shortly after they sat down on a large, flat rock and tossed their bait into the water, *Kate's* shrill, deafening screams filled Betsy's ears once again.

Teary-eyed Betsy turned to Joshua and asked him to release her from their engagement. Their hearts sank. After a long silence, Joshua slowly removed the ring from her finger. Without saying a word, they rolled up their fishing lines and slowly walked up the hill together. When they reached the Bell property line, Betsy and Joshua walked in opposite directions. They never saw each other again.

The Bell household became quiet after Betsy and Joshua parted ways. In the early summer of 1821, *Kate* visited the Bell home once and told tell Lucy Bell that she was leaving. Before Mrs. Bell could say anything, the front door flew open and a ball of fire rolled through the doorway and into the family room, where it shot up the chimney. *Kate* was gone for the time being.

She kept her promise and returned seven years later, appearing in much the same way she appeared in 1817, yet much faster. There were scratching and clawing sounds the first night, followed by whispers the second night and *Kate's* full voice on the third night.

Much of her return visit centered on John Bell, Jr., who was then living in a house about a quarter-mile from the original Bell house. For several nights, *Kate* engaged him in deep discussions about the past, the present, and the future. Particularly interesting were her predictions of the Civil War, World War I, the Great Depression, and World War II, none of which would happen for at least another 33 years.

Kate bade farewell to John Bell, Jr. three weeks later, promising to visit John Bell's most direct descendant in 107 years. In 1935, John Bell's most direct descendant was his great-grandson, Nashville physician Dr. Charles Bailey Bell. Whether *Kate* returned in 1935 is debatable, but many feel she never left to begin with. The entity that tormented John Bell's family almost 200 years ago is believed to be the source of many paranormal encounters in the area today.

If you drive near the old Bell farm on cold, rainy nights, you can sometimes see lights gliding just above the fields. Witnesses have also seen the lights, which are similar to candles, dancing in the woods near the old Bell farm late at night.

A local cemetery has also seen its share of paranormal phenomena. In the late 1990s, a family was visiting Bellwood Cemetery when they captured a terrifying apparition on their video recorder. Walking directly behind the mother was a little boy wearing early 1800's-period clothing and clutching his right arm. Did Jerusalem get his arm scraped yet again? The family noticed the little boy's apparition several weeks later when they watched the video at home for the first time. Bellwood is the final resting place of several John Bell descendants, but Bell himself, and his immediate family, are not buried there.

Theories purporting to explain the Bell Witch legend are plentiful. Some people dismiss it as hogwash; others claim to have solved the mystery, and others continue researching the case in hopes of finding concrete evidence that either proves or disproves it.

What was Kate? Was she a supernatural entity? Were the disturbances just a hoax or cover-up? Was the legend made up? No one can honestly say, at least not at *this* point. However, one thing is for sure: *Kate* was very real to those who experienced her.

❦ EIGHT ❧

The Mystical Nolichucky River

*T*HE NOLICHUCKY RIVER RUNS WESTWARD FROM THE Blue Ridge Mountains of North Carolina to the French Broad River in Tennessee, following a 150-mile course through the region's roughest terrain and deepest gorges. The Nolichucky's fierce current and deep holes have earned a daunting reputation for taking the lives of those who venture too far from its banks.

As one might guess, the ghosts of those who succumbed to the treacherous river's many perils often roam its banks and the woods nearby. For years, tourists and locals alike have encountered phantom ghost lights, eerie sounds, and ghostly apparitions along the notorious river.

Near the town of Erwin, Tennessee, the specter of a young woman emerges from the woods and walks to the water's edge, where she promptly disappears. The nude apparition, who follows the same pattern each night she appears, is oblivious to onlookers. On one occasion, campers mistook her for a swimmer and tried talking to

her when she walked past their campfire. They realized something was amiss when she ignored them and kept walking. When she reached the water's edge, she disappeared into thin air. Terrified, the campers threw down their eating utensils and fled the area. They returned for their belongings a week later.

Mike Gregory, who often camps along the river by himself, saw the apparition once in 1989 and twice in 2003. He says the encounters were like watching a movie three times in a row. Everything about the apparition, even her footsteps, was identical each time he saw her. Despite his frightening encounters with the apparition, Gregory says she is harmless.

Three well-known legends attempt to explain the apparition. A Native American legend says she was a Native American girl who jumped into the river from a high bluff and landed in roughly a foot of water, which killed her instantly. She had miscalculated the location of a deep hole. Another legend states that she was an early white settler who fell into the river and drowned while being chased through the woods by Native Americans.

The most popular legend tells of a young couple whose late night swimming escapade ended in tragedy. As they stood in the river hugging and kissing, they became so wrapped up in the moment that they unknowingly moved themselves a good distance away from the bank. They opened their eyes and found themselves standing in shoulder-deep water at the edge of the river's strong undercurrent. Before they could turn around, the young woman slipped on a submerged rock. The swift current carried her petite body downstream, eventually lodging her between two large rocks at the bottom of the river. Unable to free herself, the woman's lungs quickly filled with water and she died.

Whether the apparition is a Native American, an early white settler, or a relatively modern girl consumed by passion, no one can be sure. Legends attempting to explain her origin and the manner of her death are nearly impossible to verify. Rest assured that she is quite real, however; too many people have seen her. Although she is the Nolichucky River's most prominent ghost, she has some stiff competition only a few miles upriver, where lurks the ghost of an angler who drowned in a deep hole.

Local legend says the angler was wading in shallow water and fishing for trout when he accidentally stepped into a deep hole. The man tried to swim out of the hole, but water had filled his hip waders and weighted him down. After paddling his arms to no avail, he panicked and tried to remove his waders. Unfortunately, it was too late; he drowned before he could get them off.

Since then, people have spotted the doomed angler standing near the deep hole. Unlike his female counterpart ten miles down the river, he seems to be aware of his surroundings; he even waves to people on occasion. He disappears into the deep hole after waving, which leads many to believe his friendly wave is a farewell gesture.

One person he waved to, the leader of a whitewater rafting expedition, dove into the water and tried to rescue him when he disappeared. While searching the river's bottom for the missing angler, the rafter came upon a hole that looked to be ten feet wide and twice as deep. After returning to the surface for air, he plunged into the deep hole and began feeling his way around the bottom. As he ran his hands through the silt and muck, his fingers slid across the top of a round object that was buried in the silt. After he dislodged the mysterious object, he ran his hand over it and realized he was holding a human skull.

He quickly dropped the skull and swam to shore, where he ran to the nearest road and summoned help. A search of the hole by authorities turned up a full human skeleton and an old, mud-covered pair of hip waders with a rusty stringer of fish skeletons attached to it.

The rafter's grisly discovery tends to validate the legend about an angler drowning in a deep hole, many years ago, but it doesn't explain what happened to the angler who disappeared five minutes earlier. Many believe he was the ghost of the angler who had drowned many years ago, whose remains were found in the deep hole.

Apparitions of drowned anglers and swimmers aren't the only phenomena encountered along the infamous Nolichucky River. The surrounding land's supernatural history dates back almost 500 years.

Resting on the side of Rich Mountain in Unicoi County, Tennessee, nearly 800 feet above the river, is a giant cluster of rocks that is said to miraculously transform into the face of the devil on moonlit nights. The Juan Pardo Expedition, who named it *La Espejo De El Diablo*, first documented the spot in 1567. Two centuries later, white settlers began calling it *The Devil's Looking Glass*, which they said was a literal translation of the older, Spanish name. The early Cherokees, who hunted deer by herding them atop Rich Mountain and forcing them over the edge of The Devil's Looking Glass, believed the holes and narrow crevices along the steep drop-offs harbored evil spirits.

The Nolichucky is also home to a group of phantom *ghost lights* that glide up and down its banks late at night. The whitish yellow lights measure about two feet in diameter each, and travel just above the water's surface in groups of five to seven. The lights are bright when they flare, but their luminosity decreases with time. They eventually fade into the darkness.

Although the lights appear at random locations along the river, their behavior pattern is very consistent. They flare at Random Point A, then glide slowly – about five miles per hour – to Random Point B, where they turn around and glide back to Random Point A. The process then starts over. The distance between the two points depends on their location, which changes each night the lights appear. On most nights, the points are less than three river miles apart. The lights don't make a set number of passes between the random points. They could make twenty passes, or they could make only one pass and quickly fade away.

Night anglers have seen the phantom lights on several occasions. They appear far away at first, and then move closer, eventually passing the anglers and continuing up or down the river. The lights usually pass the anglers again within thirty minutes, traveling in the opposite direction.

Despite their predictable behavior, it's impossible to

predict *when* the lights will appear. They might appear two nights in a row, and then not reappear for a month. Like other phenomena along the Nolichucky River, the ghost lights give rise to speculation about their origin.

The most popular theory suggests the presence of *methane*, a luminous gas that is sometimes called, "swamp gas." Proponents believe concentrations of methane illuminate under certain conditions and create a "ghost light" effect. Critics argue that the number and size of the phantom lights has remained consistent, and that the area is not conducive to methane, which typically forms in empty ponds, garbage dumps, and low-lying wetlands.

Whether it's the devil's face, phantom ghost lights, ghosts who fish for trout, or ghosts who skinny-dip, those who visit the infamous Nolichucky River stand a good chance of encountering the paranormal. In a region so deeply rooted in legends and folklore, it's difficult to determine the origin and purpose of each ghost. We have only legends to go by, so let's enjoy them and draw our own conclusions.

❧ NINE ❧

Voodoo on the Bayou

URING THE EARLY 1700'S, THOUSANDS OF SLAVES were shipped from Africa to a chain of islands in the Caribbean called the Dominican Republic, where they became workers on sugar farms owned by French settlers.

While there, the slaves kept with their native African religious practices, which included ancestral worship and the use of amulets and charms. Over time, the slaves incorporated new religious practices that included worshipping nature and serving up offerings to the *Loa*, which they believed were intermediaries between the Creator and humanity. The resulting mixture of native African religious practices with the newer, island-based religious practices became known as Voodoo, which was largely confined to the Dominican Republic.

In contrast, slaves who lived in New Orleans didn't come to the area by way of the Dominican Republic. They came directly from Africa and brought with them a vast knowledge of herbs, poisons, and spells used in their native country's religious practices.

These two major slave groups, one being from the

Dominican Republic and the other being from New Orleans, came together in the early 1800's when slave revolts forced the French and their slaves away from the Dominican Republic. Most fled to New Orleans, where they integrated with the slaves who had come directly from Africa.

By 1815, New Orleans had become a *spiritual melting pot* where island worship practices that emphasized the occult met with African worship practices that emphasized ancestral worship and the use of charms and spells. The resulting mélange of Voodoo and native African religious practices became known as *Louisiana Voodoo*.

By the early 1830's, New Orleans had become home to more than fifteen *Voodoo queens* who presided over Voodoo rituals and ceremonies. Mostly of Creole and African descent, these powerful women were feared and respected because of their ability to use the occult.

One Voodoo queen in particular, Marie Laveau, stood apart from the others. Described as tall and statuesque with curly dark hair and reddish skin, she captured the attention of Voodoo practitioners, slaves, the clergy, and the city's most well to do citizens. In time, she would become the city's most powerful Voodoo queen.

Classified as a free person of color, Marie was the daughter of a Creole plantation owner and his slave mistress. She reportedly had French, Spanish, African, and Indian blood. She grew up in New Orleans, where she married Jacques Paris, a carpenter, in 1819. Soon after their marriage, Paris mysteriously disappeared and Marie, then 25, began calling herself *The Widow Paris*. She became a hairdresser and, in 1826, took up residence with Christophe Glapion.

Marie's job often took her inside the homes of New Orleans' most prominent citizens. A strong bond of trust developed between Marie and her elite clientele.

The women confessed their most personal secrets to her and kept her apprised of the latest scandals and goings-on at the upper crux of society. A bond also developed between Marie and the household servants, who regularly informed her about private matters they had heard their masters discuss. Marie knew everything about every family, politician, and social circle in New Orleans.

It wasn't long before she was telling fortunes and creating charms, potions, and hexes in her home. She also performed exorcisms and conducted sacrifice rituals. Regardless of the problem at hand, Marie always had a solution that worked. Her inevitable rise to power would soon begin.

Marie lived near Congo Square, a piece of open land behind the French Quarter where slaves gathered on Sunday afternoons to socialize and participate in African tribal dances. The dances weren't Voodoo dances in the strictest sense, but they incorporated Voodoo culture. For that reason, Voodoo queens were asked to lead the dances. Marie didn't like the arrangement because it allowed other Voodoo queens to be at the center of attention. She neither liked nor wanted competition.

Her carefully thought out strategy of always arriving early and alluring the spectators soon paid off. She became the crowd favorite, and later, the sole leader. Despite her success at Congo Square, Marie grew discontent because other Voodoo queens were living in New Orleans; her desire was to lead the city's Voodoo community by herself. To do that, she would have to eliminate her competition.

Over the next three years, Marie disposed of the other Voodoo queens by hexing them or by beating them physically until they agreed to either step down or leave the city altogether. One by one, the other Voodoo queens succumbed to Marie's relentless attacks, making her the city's most powerful Voodoo figure.

She soon began leading the St. John's Eve Voodoo rituals on the shore of Bayou St. John. These dusk-to-dawn rituals, which took place each June, included drums, bonfires, dancing, orgies, and animal sacrifices. At the center was a giant snake used to ritualize the snake spirit, *Li Grand Zombi*. Marie also led secret Voodoo ceremonies on the shores of nearby Lake Pontchartrain.

Although she wielded her power mercilessly, and was even considered malevolent by some accounts, Marie had a benevolent side as well. She cared for the poor, the sick, and the downtrodden, providing love and compassion when society wouldn't. Her extensive charity work at local infirmaries is even recognized today.

Not only was Marie a Voodoo queen, she also was a devout Catholic. Her Catholic affiliation was the driving force behind the Virgin Mary's being accepted into the Voodoo religion and becoming Loa. Priests looked upon Marie favorably because she encouraged her followers to attend Catholic mass regularly and incorporate Catholicism into their Voodoo practices.

Marie occasionally used her political influence to save innocent people from the gallows. Such was the case when a young Creole man was charged with murder and the evidence against him was overwhelming. His father sought Marie's help, promising to give her anything she wanted if she would change the trial's outcome. Hours before the trial was scheduled to begin, she made her way to the courthouse and planted several charms throughout the courtroom and in Judge Caponage's chambers.

When the trial got underway, witness after witness took the stand and testified against the young man, insisting he had killed another young man during an altercation. He seemed guilty beyond the shadow of a doubt, but for reasons unknown, he was acquitted of the charge and left the courthouse a free man. In return for Marie's favor, his father gave her a house at 152 Rue St. Ann (now called St. Ann Street) in the French Quarter, where she lived up until her death.

Marie Laveau reigned supreme over New Orleans' Voodoo circles until 1869 when, at the age of 75, she led her last Voodoo ceremony and announced her retirement. She continued to work privately with hospital patients and prisoners until 1875. She died on June 15, 1881 at her home on Rue St. Ann.

Despite obituary information that appeared in local newspapers the following day, many New Orleans residents insisted that Marie was still alive and walking the streets of the French Quarter. Some even suggested that she possessed the gift of eternal youth. The woman who was seen walking the streets was probably Marie's daughter, Marie Philomene Laveau Glapion, who bore a striking resemblance to her. When the elder Marie became confined to her house in 1875, her daughter stepped in and continued many of her activities.

A Voodoo queen in her own right, Marie's daughter took over the St. John's Eve rituals on Bayou St. John and led many other rituals throughout the area. Despite her many successes, her reputation as a Voodoo queen paled in comparison to her mother's reputation. The last of the elder Marie's fifteen children, "Marie Laveau II" died in 1897 after suffering a heart attack while attending a ball.

Marie Laveau's final resting place has been the topic of much debate, although there is ample evidence to conclude that she is entombed at Saint Louis Cemetery #1 in a family vault that bears the inscription, *Famille Veuvee Paris nee Laveau*, which translates to "The Widow Paris, born Laveau." The vault also bears the inscription, *Marie Philome Glapion, deceased June 11,*

1897, which suggests that her daughter is also entombed in the family vault.

With its vast expanse of above ground burial vaults, St. Louis Cemetery #1 is sometimes called a "city of the dead." Standing well over six feet tall, The Laveau-

Glapion vault is visited daily by tourists and Voodoo practitioners alike. It bears numerous markings and crosses drawn by visitors using pieces of red brick taken from decaying vaults nearby. Many people denounce the practice because it amounts to vandalism of the nearby vaults.

According to legend, you will secure Marie Laveau's blessing if you draw three X-marks on the tomb, cover the marks with your hands, close your eyes, and rub your foot against the tomb three times. At the foot of the tomb are coins, flowers, bones, tobacco, and other items left in exchange for Marie's help. Can she see the items? It's a safe bet that she can because, even in death, her spiritual likeness reportedly roams the French Quarter and the dark, snake-infested bayous where she led Voodoo ceremonies for many decades.

One popular account of Marie's lingering presence is that of a man who fell asleep in St. Louis Cemetery #1 and awoke at sunrise to the sounds of Voodoo drums and people chanting. Lying on his side and with the vaults behind him, the startled man looked back and saw a group of misty, human-like figures dancing in the middle of the cemetery. They were being led by a tall woman with a large snake wrapped around her body. Thought to be Marie Laveau and her followers, the apparition and sounds quickly faded away when the man asked the dance leader to help him. He had apparently forgotten to leave an offering at Marie's tomb.

Another account, which dates back to the 1930's, says that a customer sitting in a drugstore near St. Louis Cemetery #1 saw the pharmacist suddenly drop a bottle of pills, run to the back storage area, and quickly bolt the door behind him.

A well-dressed, elderly woman had just come through the front door. Having seen what the terrified pharmacist did, the woman laughed hysterically as she walked over to the counter and sat down next to the customer. After regaining her composure, she turned to him and asked politely, "Do you know who I am?"

"No, ma'am, I don't," the man answered.

Then, in a more aggressive tone, the woman asked again, "Do you know who I am?"

"No, Ma'am, I don't. I'm terribly sorry!"

Disappointed by the man's answer, she slapped him across the face and quickly reached into the black bag she was carrying. Before he could turn away from her, she pulled out a pinch of brownish powder and flicked it into his face. Overcome by the powder's strong odor, the man buckled, fell to the floor, and lost consciousness.

Waking up a minute later, he looked up and saw the woman floating through the air and gravitating slowly toward the front door. She floated out the door and up through the air outside. The terrified man walked outside and watched her float over the graveyard wall, where she disappeared. He walked back inside the drugstore and saw the pharmacist standing behind the counter. He then accused the pharmacist of lacing his soft drink with some type of drug. Still trembling, the pharmacist denied the man's allegation and told him that he had just encountered the Voodoo queen, Marie Laveau.

In a similar case, a local man claimed that he was slapped by Marie Laveau as he walked past St. Louis Cemetery #1 on a warm June afternoon. He said Marie's ghost was easily recognizable because she always wore a *tignon*, a seven-knotted handkerchief, around her neck. The elderly woman who allegedly slapped him was wearing a tignon around her neck, also. The incident occurred in latter June, the period during which Marie allegedly returns to life each year and presides over the Voodoo ceremony held on St. John's Eve.

The house where Marie Laveau lived for most of her

adult life was razed in 1903. Nevertheless, many people claim to see the ghosts of Marie and her followers participating in Voodoo ceremonies inside the house that now occupies the spot. Others claim to see Marie dancing along the shores of Bayou St. John and Lake Pontchartrain.

Marie Laveau is a figure shrouded in mystery. Regardless of whether she was evil, benevolent, or a mixture of both, she was a very strong, independent, and spiritual woman who earned the respect of people from all walks of life. She forged her mark on the Voodoo religion and the city of New Orleans. Visit her tomb if you dare, but make sure to leave her something, lest she will forge her mark – whether benevolent, malevolent, or indifferent – on you.

❧ TEN ❧

The Curse of Lorenzo Dow

*I*N THE WOODS NEAR SYLVANIA, GEORGIA, LAY THE RUINS of Jacksonboro, a once-thriving frontier town where rowdiness ran rampant and the whiskey bottle reigned supreme. In 1821, an unexpected series of events reduced Jacksonboro to a ghost town, and many believe the curse of a traveling preacher is to blame.

Chartered in 1799 and located in rural Georgia between Macon and Savannah, Jacksonboro was the center of commerce for area planters, trappers, and loggers. The quintessential town of its day, Jacksonboro had a blacksmith's shop and general store, a hotel, a church, two saloons, a whiskey store, and a mortuary.

The town's residents labored by day and played by night, often crowding into saloons and drinking the whiskey barrels dry before closing time. Drunken brawls kept the doctor, and sometimes the undertaker, very busy. Recalling the history of Jacksonboro in his 1849 book, *Statistics of the State of Georgia*, George White writes, "The place had a very bad character. In the mornings after drunken frolics and fights, you could see children picking up eyeballs in tea saucers."

Despite its reputation for being a rough and rowdy town, Jacksonboro was in good financial condition because its businesses met the needs of its citizens. They offered employment as well as a place where their employees could spend their hard-earned money; a citizen who worked at the general store could later spend their earnings at the general store when buying for their family. In 1821, things began to change for the bustling whiskey town.

Many of its businesses failed despite their having scores of loyal customers and a steady stream of business. Fire and tornado damage had wiped out most of their profits, and many townspeople were left without jobs. Jacksonboro had not experienced a fire or a tornado in its 21 years of existence, but the year 1821 brought with it several fires, tornadoes, and floods, all of which occurred over a seven-month period.

Jacksonboro's sudden onslaught of bad luck didn't end with its businesses; homes and farms were affected as well. Two of the area's biggest houses were ravaged by fire, and tornadoes destroyed four others. In another, rather bizarre case, a house in good condition fell to pieces during a light thunderstorm. Many crops died that year despite an overabundance of rain, and flash flooding along Beaver Dam Creek swept away several residents and their livestock.

Mounting financial problems forced businesses and residents to relocate and start anew. The once-thriving town of Jacksonboro soon became nothing but a ghost town in the piney Georgia wilderness. The cause of the events that led to the town's demise remains a mystery, but many place the blame on a traveling preacher who became angry and placed a curse on the town. *The Curse of Lorenzo Dow* is one of the oddest events and most enduring legends in Georgia history.

LORENZO DOW.

Born in Connecticut, Lorenzo Dow traveled the United States and Europe in the early 1800's, preaching to anyone who would listen. A vigilant, hardnosed crusader for the gospel, Dow delivered his hellfire-and-brimstone sermons with such fervor and conviction that many people feared and hated him; some even labeled him a criminal. His reputation earned him the nickname, "Crazy Dow," to which he gladly answered.

Dow's evangelical strategy was to arrive in a town and

pass out handbills until nightfall. Once a large crowd had gathered, he would begin preaching. His fervent sermons lasted for hours, and he publicly scolded anyone who dared to walk away before he finished. Dow's tall and slender figure, long hair, and scruffy beard made him stand out in any crowd, which was a problem because angry mobs often pursued him. For that reason, he never stuck around after he preached. He would leave quickly, spend the night with another preacher, and leave town early the next morning.

Despite his harsh reputation, Lorenzo Dow was the world's most prolific evangelist at the time; his name was a household word all across America, Canada, and Europe. In 1820, he had occasion to visit the South and preach to Georgia's General Assembly. Not liking what he saw in Georgia, he decided to stay several weeks and bring his message to the masses. One fall day, without giving prior notice to anyone, Dow showed up in Jacksonboro.

News of his presence spread like wildfire in a dry pine thicket, setting the little town ablaze with gossip, hatred, and resentment. The church offered Dow their building, and by nightfall, a large crowd had gathered to hear him preach. Another crowd – a drunken mob – had formed at the nearby whiskey store. Their plan was to disrupt Dow's sermon and force him out of town.

The drunken mob made their way to the church soon after Dow began preaching. Kicking open the front door, they rushed down the aisle to the pulpit and began yelling obscenities at him. He ignored them and continued his sermon. Two mobsters then pulled rotten eggs from their pockets and threw them at Dow. Once again, he continued as if nothing had happened. The angry mob stumbled up the aisle, slammed the door behind them, and staggered back to the whiskey store.

When his sermon concluded, Dow politely excused

himself and made his way to the whiskey store. After kicking down the front door, he jerked an axe away from a man and split open two barrels of whiskey. Then, without saying a word, he turned around and walked out. The furious mob rushed out the door behind him and began looking for a suitable tree from which he could hang.

Luck was on Dow's side, however. Seaborn Goodall, a church member, approached the mob and made them a deal. In return for their allowing Dow to spend the night at his house, he would make him leave town at first light. Surprisingly, they agreed to Goodall's terms and returned to the whiskey store, where they promptly opened a new barrel of whiskey. All night long, the mobsters sipped whiskey and talked about their strong hatred for Dow, cursing him with every breath and becoming angrier by the minute.

Just before dawn, they mounted their horses and rode to Seaborn Goodall's farm. As the drunken mob waited in the front yard for Dow to leave, they decided they would torch Goodall's house if he didn't go through with the deal he had made them. A minute later, and much to their surprise, Lorenzo Dow emerged from the house and began walking in the direction of Beaver Dam Creek, which was Jacksonboro's southern boundary.

The mob followed closely behind, pelting him with rocks, tomatoes, and rotten eggs. As soon as Dow had crossed the small bridge over Beaver Dam Creek, he stopped and turned around. Standing his ground, he gazed at the mob for a full minute, never blinking an eye. He then removed his shoes and shook the dust from them. He put them back on and gazed at the mob once again.

Speaking in a very polite and diplomatic tone, Dow pronounced a curse on the town of Jacksonboro and its citizens, with the exception of Seaborn Goodall. The mob erupted in laughter as Lorenzo Dow, the most famous person ever to visit Jacksonboro, turned around and walked into the wilderness. He was not seen or heard from again in those parts. In less than a year, Jacksonboro began experiencing the problems that led to its ultimate demise.

Lorenzo Dow traveled over 200,000 miles in his career. He preached in the United States, Canada, England, Ireland, and the West Indies. His permanent home was Washington, D.C., where he died in 1834 at the age of 57.

Aside from a few old foundation stones scattered throughout the woods, all that remains of Jacksonboro today is a modest, two-story white clapboard house that sits off a dirt road in rural Screven County, Georgia. Land records show that the house and surrounding land once belonged to... Seaborn Goodall.

✑ ELEVEN ✏

The Bragg Ghost Light

T HE "BIG THICKET" IS A DARK AND DENSELY WOODED area of southeast Texas that occupies much of Hardin, Liberty, Tyler, Jasper, and Polk Counties. Comprising nearly 85,000 acres and bounded by two rivers and a bayou, the mostly remote area is sometimes called, "the biological crossroads of North America," because of the many plant and animal species that inhabit its abundant thickets, soggy marshes, and dense forests. More than five thousand species of flowering plants and ferns, as well as a healthy population of alligators and venomous snakes, make The Big Thicket their home.

The Big Thicket is also home to a few small towns that evolved from the local oil and lumber industries in the late nineteenth century. Many of the early towns were abandoned when the industries slowed in the early 1930's; other towns either continued to function on their own or became suburbs of nearby Beaumont, Texas.

The Big Thicket's dark forests, with their stagnant, weed-filled marshes, conjure thoughts of missing persons, larger-than-life creatures, and other entities that go bump in the night. Deeply rooted in folklore, the area abounds with tales of hunters vanishing, bodies resting in unmarked graves, people being burned alive, and giant, Bigfoot-like creatures roaming the thickets and marshes.

Whether such tales are true – or to what extent they're true – is anyone's guess; many find them hard to believe. On the contrary, most find it easy to believe in the existence of a ghostly light that appears along a dark, tree-lined road in the heart of The Big Thicket, and for good reason. The mysterious light can be seen easily; even *National Geographic Magazine* has photographed it. Its origin and purpose, however, are a century-old mystery.

Known as the "Bragg Ghost Light," or the "Saratoga Light," the mysterious glow appears along Old Bragg Road in Hardin County. Lying fifteen miles west of Kountze, Texas, the two-lane dirt road runs south from the ghost town of Bragg Station to the Saratoga community, for a distance of about seven miles.

Often called, "Ghost Road," Old Bragg Road dates back to 1901 when the Santa Fe Railroad laid tracks through the area to carry lumber, cattle, oil, and passengers to the nearby city of Beaumont. The tracks connected to a branch line that was laid between Bragg Station and Saratoga for the purpose of transporting oil and lumber. By 1934, however, the area's oil and lumber industries had dried up. The branch line was removed and its abandoned right-of-way became Old Bragg Road.

People have seen the eerie light all along the road at different times of the night. On some nights, observers come at dusk and wait nearly all night for the light to appear. On other nights, the light appears much sooner or, in some cases, doesn't appear at all.

The light is yellowish when it flares, and then it fades

into white, usually over the course of an hour. Some have observed the light turn reddish orange after it has been visible longer than an hour. From a distance, it appears to flicker and swing back and forth in a pattern similar to a lantern being waved by a train conductor.

In most cases, the light appears in the distance and slowly moves toward the observer, disappearing shortly before it reaches them. A local legend says the light will disappear if you honk your car's horn; however, many observers have reported the opposite effect. One group said the light actually *followed* their vehicle after they honked the horn. Another observer said the light landed on his car's roof and began making strange noises after he honked the horn.

No one knows when the Bragg Ghost Light was seen for the first time, but some locals say it predates the railroad. People saw the light in the woods and went looking for it as early as the 1890's. Many thought the light was a prank being played by children who brought lanterns into the woods. Sightings occurred more often when the railroad's right-of-way became a county road; more people had access to the area, hence, there were more chances to see the mysterious light. By 1960, the ghost light had become a regional tourist attraction, due in large part to a series of front-page stories in the local newspaper, *The Kountze News*, which were picked up by newspapers throughout the region.

Sightings of the mysterious light continue today with curiosity seekers, paranormal investigators, scientists, and photographers coming from all over the country to witness the phenomenon. Although most people who see the light agree that it's real, no one seems to know what it really is. The paranormal community offers up several theories, as do the scientific and religious communities.

One paranormal theory suggests that a railroad worker was decapitated in a tragic accident on the branch line many years ago, and that the ghost light represents his lantern swinging back and forth as he looks for his missing head. The same theory has been used to explain railroad-related ghost lights in at least two dozen states. Another paranormal theory, which is rooted in local folklore, suggests that the light comes from an ethereal fire pan being carried by a hunter who became lost in the thicket many years ago. He is still searching for a way out.

Another theory tells of immigrant workers who were hired to cut the branch line's right-of-way and lay the tracks. When they finished the job, their greedy supervisor decided to kill them rather than pay them. He allegedly buried them in unmarked graves in the nearby woods, and their lost souls haunt the old railroad right-of-way.

Members of the scientific community argue that the light is most likely a concentration of luminous swamp gas, or perhaps a reflection of vehicle lights in the distance. Scientists also have suggested that the mysterious light is *foxfire*, in which bioluminescence is created by a species of wood-decaying fungi under certain conditions.

A preacher once proclaimed that the light is an omen signifying the end of the world. Another preacher said God placed the light in order to light the way out of the dangerous thicket. A rural church declared that those who see the mysterious light are guilty of worshiping a false God, and will burn in hell for it.

Local history also offers some possible explanations for the Bragg Ghost Light, although most are along the lines of folklore rather than history. One theory suggests that some early Spanish conquistadors hid gold in the thicket but failed to return for it. The light allegedly signifies the buried treasure's presence. Another theory, based on history to some extent, suggests that the Kaiser

Burnout, one of the Civil War's lesser-known events, is responsible for the light.

Some of the men who lived in The Big Thicket area during the Civil War refused to fight for the Confederacy. Known as "Jayhawkers," the men sought refuge deep in the thicket where they couldn't be found easily. In the early spring of 1865, Confederate Captain James Kaiser flushed them out by setting fire to the thicket. The fire that ensued destroyed 3,000 acres of the thicket and claimed the lives of several Jayhawkers. Some say the mysterious Bragg Ghost Light is a remnant of the raging fire, which supposedly never burned completely out. Others claim the light is the ghost of a Jayhawker who perished in the fire.

The mysterious and sometimes elusive Bragg Ghost Light continues to baffle, intrigue, and fascinate paranormal researchers, scientists, prophets, and historians. Whether it's a decapitated railroader, an omen signaling the world's end, a concentration of luminous gas, or a lasting ember from the Civil War, no one can say; but everyone who has seen the light – even National Geographic – says it is real.

Perhaps someday, someone will be able to explain what the light really is and why it's there. Should you decide to visit The Big Thicket in the meantime, make sure to carry a flashlight, pray for forgiveness, and lay off your horn.

❧ TWELVE ❧

Cedarhurst Mansion

*T*HE NORTH ALABAMA TOWN OF HUNTSVILLE IS HOME to NASA's Marshall Space Flight Center. College graduates, mostly PhD's, flock to Huntsville and land jobs at NASA or one of the area's many high-tech companies. In addition to its being well represented in the scientific community, Huntsville also stands out in the paranormal community, due in large part to Cedarhurst Mansion. Cedarhurst is home to one of the region's most prominent and long-standing ghost stories.

Stephen Ewing built Cedarhurst in 1823 for his wife, Mary. With its fifteen-inch outer walls and two grand staircases, the stately mansion was home to several generations of the Ewing family. The mansion's most prominent ghost is that of Sally Carter, a young girl who died in an upstairs bedroom back in the 1800's.

Sally came to Cedarhurst in the summer of 1837 to visit her aunt, Mary Ewing, and she fell in love with the place. The house was big; the Ewings made her feel at home; and the beautiful countryside was a natural playground that any fifteen-year-old girl would love. Sally eventually talked her family into letting her stay longer. Instead of returning home at the end of summer, she would stay at Cedarhurst several months and then return home for Christmas.

The fall of 1837 was unseasonably cold, but neither cold winds nor early snowfalls could stop Sally from taking hikes through the woods and riding horses on the grounds of the massive plantation. Things went well for Sally until she came down with pneumonia in the latter part of November. She spent the next five days in her upstairs bedroom, wheezing and suffering until she finally succumbed to the illness. She was buried in a small, fenced-in family plot near the mansion. Although her trip was cut short in the physical sense, Sally's presence is still felt at Cedarhurst.

One of the best-known encounters with Sally took place in 1919 when a young boy came to visit relatives at Cedarhurst. The boy slept in an upstairs bedroom near the room where Sally had died. One night was particularly stormy. Every time he began to doze off, he was awakened by crackling thunder or the sound of tree limbs beating against the window when the wind blew them. After tossing and turning for hours, he finally went to sleep. He was awakened an hour later by something he had never seen before: a tall, young girl with long dark hair, standing over his bed.

Terrified, the boy closed his eyes and lay completely still for the better part of five minutes. Then, gradually, he opened his eyes and looked around the room. It was very dark; all he could see was the area beside his bed. After letting his eyes adjust to the darkness, he gazed around the room and saw nothing; everything was just as he had left it. He dismissed the young girl's visit as a dream and fell back asleep.

Later that night, he awoke and saw the girl standing over his bed again. In a polite but very urgent tone, she told him that the wind had toppled her gravestone and that she wanted him to prop it back up. The boy blinked his eyes and the apparition vanished. He felt awake at that point, but he wasn't sure if he had really been awake a few seconds earlier, when he saw the girl. He dismissed this second incident as a dream, also.

While eating breakfast the next morning, the boy told his relatives about the strange dreams he had experienced the night before. His uncle said that there was an old, unkept cemetery in a thicket not far from the mansion, and that no one had been buried there in at least fifty years. His curiosity piqued, the boy put on his boots and went outside for a walk on the grounds.

Knowing that a graveyard existed on the property, he couldn't help but think about his dreams and what the young girl had told him. Were they really dreams, or did he see the ghost of young girl whose gravestone had been toppled by high winds the night before? He felt compelled to find the answer to his question, but he was terrified by the mere thought of finding an overturned gravestone with a young girl's name on it. If he did, how could he be sure it wasn't a coincidence? On the other hand, if he didn't visit the graveyard at all, would the ghost – assuming that one existed – reappear to him?

After walking a short while, he came upon the thicket his uncle had told him about at breakfast. Carefully pushing limbs, weeds, and thorns out of his way, he inched his way through the dense undergrowth. Ten minutes later, he spotted five old gravestones in the middle of a cedar-lined clearing at the crest of a small hill. He took a deep breath, looked in all directions, and slowly made his way into the clearing.

A thin layer of moss and a spattering of dried tree sap covered each gravestone. He studied each gravestone carefully, running his fingers over the moss-covered inscriptions and trying to make out the letters. The names weren't familiar, and none of the stones had been toppled, so he decided to leave.

As the boy left the clearing, he couldn't help but notice a gravestone lying face down on the ground next to him. He had walked past it on his way into the clearing, but he had apparently overlooked it. The stone looked like it had been pushed over with a great deal of force. He slid his hands underneath the stone and gently pushed it upward. He noticed that the ground underneath the toppled gravestone was wet, which indicated that the stone had been toppled during the storm the night before.

Terrified, the anxious boy slowly turned the gravestone around, closed his eyes briefly, and then read the inscription. It read: *Sally Carter - 1822-1837*. After making sure that Sally's gravestone was upright and firmly planted in the ground, he left the cemetery. He remained at Cedarhurst for two more weeks and never encountered Sally again.

Toppled gravestones are but a small part of the phenomena associated with Sally Carter and Cedarhurst Mansion. A playful ghost who can be downright annoying at times, Sally has been seen and heard all over the mansion and the grounds.

One popular account tells of a guard at Cedarhurst who heard footsteps upstairs one night. No one else was inside the mansion. When her shift ended, she noticed that some of her money was missing. She searched the mansion for nearly an hour while someone's footsteps followed closely behind her. Her flashlight going dim, she abandoned her search and walked back to the guardhouse. Her flashlight lit back up as soon as she opened the guardhouse's door, and it shined directly on the money she had been looking for. The guard said jokingly, "Thank you, Sally!" Female laughter filled the room.

In another case, a man spent the night at the mansion

and slept in Sally's room. He told of doors opening and closing by themselves, lights turning on and off by themselves, and bedcovers being pulled off the bed. He said the phenomena were preceded by the sound of footsteps coming down the hall. Others who have slept in Sally's room tell about waking up in the middle of the night and seeing the rocking chair rock by itself.

Sally probably likes jewelry as much as she likes light switches and rocking chairs. For years, women have found their pearl necklaces broken and the pearls scattered all over the mansion. As one might imagine, they blame Sally. On one occasion, a woman even found her necklace hanging from a curtain rod. When she reached up to retrieve the necklace, it broke before she could touch it. All the pearls fell off, and a female, presumably Sally, laughed hysterically.

Sally Carter's popularity grew over the years, with people coming from all over northern Alabama to visit her grave and possibly catch a glimpse of her on the grounds. Her grave became such a popular destination that, over time, visitors etched a path through the thicket. Vandals also visited Sally's grave; they often moved her headstone around the graveyard and left empty beer cans and cigarette packs behind.

In 1982, the graves of Mary Ewing and her three children were relocated to an undisclosed location in Maple Hill Cemetery to make way for a real estate development on the former Cedarhurst grounds. What about Sally Carter's grave?

According to reports, the contractor responsible for relocating the family plot said that Sally's grave was empty. He theorized that the true location of her grave couldn't be determined because vandals had moved her headstone so many times. Others insist that Sally's grave was moved to Maple Hill Cemetery many years earlier, although there is no known record of it. It's very likely that Sally Carter's remains and wooden casket had fully deteriorated by 1982. The practice of preserving dead bodies didn't begin in the United States until the Civil War, nearly thirty years after Sally's death.

Today, the former Cedarhurst Plantation is an upscale, gated community. The mansion, which remains intact, is being used as a private clubhouse. To enter the property or tour the mansion, you must either live there or know someone who does. It is rumored that Sally still lives there; maybe she will let you in.

❧ THIRTEEN ❧

The Waving Girl of Savannah

*T*HROUGHOUT THE 1800'S AND EARLY 1900'S, THE harbor at Savannah, Georgia was among the busiest harbors in the country. With an abundance of rice, indigo, and cotton nearby, ships loaded up with goods at Savannah and sailed for Genoa, Liverpool, South Africa, and other far-away ports. Smaller vessels carried tobacco, potatoes, and island cotton between Savannah and other coastal ports. Savannah Harbor also boasted one of the largest fishing fleets in the Atlantic Ocean.

About five miles downstream from the harbor is Elba Island, which marks its entrance. All ocean-going vessels using the harbor must pass the island. Now dotted with businesses and industrial sites, Elba Island was relatively uninhabited in the nineteenth century, boasting little more than a lighthouse and a modest cottage for the lightkeeper to live in.

Florence Martus and her older brother, George, moved to Elba Island in 1887 when he became the lightkeeper.

They lived in a small cottage near the river. Small cargo and fishing vessels often stopped at Elba Island to make final preparations for entering the Harbor. Florence and her brother became friends with many of the local sailors and commercial fishermen.

Florence, who was then 18, began dating a young sailor, Andrew, who was from Beaufort, South Carolina. Andrew had worked several years as a deckhand on a small cargo steamer that ran between Savannah and Charleston, South Carolina. Knowing the steamer by sight and by the sound of its whistle, Florence would rush to the river's edge whenever it passed. She would wave her handkerchief in the wind and Andrew would wave back. In love with each other, Florence and Andrew became engaged.

They had been engaged only a month when they received some bad news one afternoon. Andrew's company had assigned him to an ocean-going cargo vessel, which meant he would be sailing the high seas for weeks or possibly even months at a time. Although his pay would be much better, he would be expected to sail away on a moment's notice. It would be impossible to know how long each trip would take.

A week later, Andrew was ordered to report to Charleston Harbor and board the steamship, *Parkland*. The vessel would sail to Savannah and take on a load of cotton and indigo, then sail to Genoa, Italy. Reality having set in, a worried and disappointed Florence Martus promised to wait for Andrew's return no matter how long it would take.

The *Parkland* steamed past Elba Island two days later, and Florence waved to Andrew until the vessel was almost out of sight. She had wanted to kiss him a final time, but she couldn't visit the dock in Savannah because her brother was using their dingy, which was their only transportation. Later that day, just before dusk, the *Parkland* steamed past Elba Island a second time; she was bound for Italy. Florence and Andrew waved to each other once again. On the verge of tears, Florence promised herself that she would greet every ship that passed the lighthouse until Andrew returned.

She kept her promise. Whenever a vessel would approach the lighthouse, she would scurry down to the river's edge and wave her white handkerchief in the air. At night, she would swing her lantern, much to the enjoyment of her collie dog.

Months passed and Andrew didn't return. Feeling worried and sensing betrayal, Florence asked some of the local sailors if they knew of his whereabouts. They didn't sail the high seas like Andrew, but maybe they had heard something through the grapevine, she reasoned. As it turned out, none of them had any recollection of Andrew.

For nearly half a century, Florence rushed out of her cottage and waved to every ship that passed Elba Island. She waved – with her handkerchief by day and her lantern by night – to the delight of ship captains, crews, and passengers. They often waved back, and captains even gave whistle salutes on occasion. Despite her popularity and claim to nautical fame, Florence was never happy. Andrew, her only true love, was gone.

In 1930, an aging Florence Martus moved away from Elba Island when her brother retired from his job. She died in 1943, the same year in which a cargo ship, the *SS Florence Martus*, was christened in her honor. A statue of Florence and her collie dog now stands in Morrell Park on Savannah's historic riverfront.

Did Florence Martus really leave Elba Island? Many people don't think so. For even in death, she is still seen at the water's edge waving her handkerchief and swinging her lantern, hoping that each passing ship will bring Andrew back to her.

It's difficult to pinpoint when Florence's apparition began appearing. One account dates back to 1943, when someone reported seeing her apparition walking along the shores of Elba Island the day she died. Unfortunately, the account can't be verified because the only witness died long ago and left no written account of the incident. Her apparition has appeared consistently since then, sometimes once a week.

There is no mistake as to the apparition's identity; all eyewitnesses agree that it's Florence Martus. The apparition follows her pattern of waving a handkerchief during the day and swinging a lantern at night. It is seen only when ships pass the island, but not *every* time a ship passes. Apparently, Florence has decided that Andrew wouldn't be sailing on certain ships.

The apparition lasts a short time, often less than a minute, before disappearing. Those who have spotted the apparition while taking boat tours say it fades in and out, similar to the flicker of a candle.

What happened to Andrew? Records of non-commissioned sailors, such as deckhands, weren't kept very well in those days, and are nearly impossible to find now. Perhaps he found another woman in another port; perhaps he was among the many sailors who perished in fires that broke out on ships; perhaps he succumbed to an epidemic on the high seas.

If Andrew ever returns, his fiercely loyal fiancée, who is now affectionately called, "Savannah's Waving Girl," still awaits him on the spot where they saw each other for the last time.

⇜ FOURTEEN ⇝

The McRaven House

*H*OME TO NEARLY A DOZEN SPIRITS, THE MCRAVEN House in Vicksburg, Mississippi is reputed to be the state's most haunted house. Over the years, countless people have reported seeing apparitions, hearing voices, and being shoved while walking inside the house or on its grounds.

The McRaven house was built over time, in three distinct phases. The first part of McRaven was built in 1797 by Andrew Glass, and consisted of a kitchen with a bedroom above it. Known as the *Pioneer Section*, this part of the house is still intact today.

In its earliest years, McRaven served as a way station for pioneers traveling the Natchez Trace, an early footpath that connected Nashville, Tennessee with the Mississippi River. In the early 1830's, McRaven became a way station on the Trail of Tears, a migration path used to forcefully relocate 15,000 Cherokees from their homes in the East to the Oklahoma desert.

In 1836, Stephen Howard bought the house and added a dining room and a middle bedroom. In August of that year, Howard's wife, Mary Elizabeth, died in the middle bedroom while giving birth. A misty female apparition now occupies the corner of the room. Although very frightening at first sight, the apparition is harmless; it disappears after about five seconds. Mary Elizabeth Howard's deathbed still exists, as does her wedding shawl. The wedding shawl reportedly gives off so much heat that people can't touch it for long. The lamp next to her deathbed allegedly turns itself on and off.

In 1849, John Bobb purchased the house and added a hallway, a flying wing staircase, a parlor, a dressing room, and a master bedroom. Although the flying wing staircase wasn't there during Mary Elizabeth Howard's lifetime, her ghost took an instant liking to it. Visitors occasionally report seeing her apparition – the same one that haunts the middle bedroom – standing atop the staircase.

The McRaven House served as a Confederate field hospital and campsite during the Siege of Vicksburg in 1863. The house undoubtedly saw its share of mortally wounded soldiers who agonized for days, and often weeks, before their misery ended. The number of Civil War soldiers buried at McRaven is unknown, but visitors have seen them, both Union and Confederate soldiers, wandering about the grounds on several occasions.

The most prominent Civil War ghost at McRaven is that of Captain James McPherson, a Vicksburg resident who left town at the war's onset to join the Union Army. McPherson was an aide to Colonel J.H. Wilson, the officer in charge of Vicksburg after its fall in July of 1863. Because of McPherson's close ties to the area, Wilson made him the liaison between the Union Army and the residents of Vicksburg.

Despite his close ties to the area, McPherson was disliked by many of its residents. They saw him as a local boy who had betrayed them by fighting for their enemy. McPherson disappeared late one night after making his rounds. Army scouts searched for him the next morning but found nothing. He was declared missing the next day.

Colonel Wilson, while sleeping at the McRaven House two weeks later, rolled over in his bed and spotted Captain McPherson's blood-soaked, ghostly apparition sitting in a rocking chair across the room. Struggling to breathe, McPherson said a group of angry residents had killed him and disposed of his corpse in the Mississippi River. The apparition vanished before Colonel Wilson could regain his composure.

The apparition would eventually return and stay at McRaven for eternity. Wearing a Union Army uniform and sporting a bullet hole in his forehead, the ghost of Captain McPherson roams the grounds at McRaven by day and haunts the streets of Vicksburg by night.

Not long after Vicksburg fell to Union forces, John Bobb saw a group of Union soldiers picking flowers from McRaven's front lawn. He darted outside and ordered them to leave. The angry soldiers stomped and crushed the remaining flowers, then began cursing him. Bobb hurled a brick, striking a soldier in the head. The soldiers then left, but revenge was forthcoming.

Bobb reported the incident to General Henry Slocum, who promised to discipline the soldiers responsible. When Bobb returned to McRaven, 25 Union soldiers met him at the front gate. The vengeful soldiers dragged him to a nearby pond and shot him through the back of his head.

John Bobb's ghost often appears in a room just off McRaven's main foyer, watching from a distance as visitors enter the house. People have also witnessed a ghostly figure walking along the edge of the pond where Bobb was murdered. Having seen John Bobb depicted in a painting, most witnesses agree that the apparition seen in the foyer and near the pond is indeed him. Some theorize that he is watching over the foyer and nearby pond in hopes of seeing his killers and getting revenge on them.

Little is known about McRaven's ownership during the reconstruction period that followed the Civil War. John Bobb had ceased to own McRaven when he was murdered in 1863. Its next recognizable owner was William Murray, who bought the place for his family in 1882.

Five members of the Murray family died at McRaven, the last of which was William Murray's daughter, Ella, who died in 1960. A recluse who lived in the house by herself for many years, Ella rarely communicated with anyone but her doctor. She allegedly burned furniture to heat the place. Over the years, visitors have spotted her ghost standing by the stove in the kitchen. The ghost of William Murray often stands atop the flying wing staircase and greets visitors. The ghosts of his wife and daughters allegedly roam the grounds early in the morning and late in the afternoon.

In 1961, McRaven was sold to the Bradway family, who restored the aging structure and opened it to the public. The Bradway's, who didn't actually live in the house, occasionally received late-night phone calls about the lights being on at McRaven. In one case, a caller reported seeing human figures walking around inside the house after the lights mysteriously came on at 2 A.M. No one but the Bradway's, who had been asleep for hours, had keys to the place. As a rule, the lights were turned off when the house closed each afternoon.

In 1984, Leyland French purchased McRaven and made further restorations. French encountered William Murray's ghost on the staircase one night and became frightened, although he knew it wouldn't hurt him. After a second encounter with Murray's ghost, in which a desk drawer shut on his hand, French asked a local priest to bless the house. Paranormal activity in the house subsided for a spell after the priest's visit, but it eventually returned in full force.

In 1999, parapsychologists William Roll and Andrew Nichols, both professors at the State University of West Georgia, visited McRaven to investigate the many alleged ghost sightings there. Armed with an array of field instruments, they discovered and carefully analyzed a number of electromagnetic fields in and around the house. The fields, they say, break down filtering mechanisms in the brain and allow us to perceive a level of reality that's always present, although we aren't usually aware of it. Hence, the longer one lives around such fields, the more sensitive they become to the other level of reality.

Roll and Nichols also discovered a powerful energy field that radiates from a natural source beneath the house. They likened McRaven to a "storage battery," where people walk through the house or the yard and expose themselves to the energy field. In turn, their filtering mechanisms break down and they become more attuned to the other level of reality.

McRaven's dark and bloody history makes it one of the most haunted houses in Mississippi. With so much ghostly activity being reported there, and with so much energy on the property, McRaven could easily be the most haunted house in all of Dixie.

❧ FIFTEEN ❧

The Greenbrier Ghost

*T*HE BRUTAL MURDER OF A YOUNG WOMAN IN 1897 turned a rural West Virginia courtroom into a spectacle of laughter and disbelief as jurors condemned a man to prison based on the testimony of a ghost. The incident is one of the oddest events in the history of America's legal system, and one of the oddest Appalachian folktales ever told.

Known as "the wild rose of Greenbrier," Zona Heaster was born in 1876 on Little Sewell Mountain in Fayette County, West Virginia. In her adolescent years, she moved to Greenbrier County where, despite her plain appearance and timid disposition, she became quite popular with the young men. Her mother, described as a strong, God-fearing woman, carefully questioned every boy who wanted to court Zona. The sparsely populated West Virginia wilderness offered few boys from which to choose, and she insisted that her daughter court only the cream of the crop.

One day in September of 1896, Mary Heaster became irate when Zona brought home a man named Erasmus Stribbling Trout Shue. Not only was he much older than

Zona, he also had "the face and charm of the Devil," Mrs. Heaster said. Shue remained calm and polite while she bombarded him with questions, most of which she answered for him. His cool, uncanny disposition made her even more wary of him.

A quick-tempered man who stole from others and physically abused women, Trout Shue was anything but the cream of the crop. Unfortunately, his reputation hadn't followed him to Greenbrier County; Mrs. Heaster had nothing to rely on but her instinct, which later proved to be correct. She could no longer give men the benefit of the doubt. A year earlier, she had allowed Zona to court a drifter. Eight months after he had left, she gave birth to a child out of wedlock.

A drifter himself, Trout Shue was from Pocahontas County, West Virginia, where in the late 1880's he was sent to jail for stealing a horse. His then wife divorced him over the incident. In 1894, he met Lucy Tritt and married her a short time later. The couple lived with Trout's parents for several months before deciding to build a house atop Droop Mountain in nearby Greenbrier County.

Lucy went missing one afternoon while the couple was still in the process of building their house. A bear hunter found her lying face down in a nearby ravine the next morning and called authorities. Trout Shue, who had never bothered to report his wife's disappearance, told authorities that she had accidentally slipped over a cliff while being chased by a rattlesnake. The authorities, who apparently knew very little about rattlesnakes, offered Shue their condolences and left.

Shue ran out of money before he could finish building the house, so he took a job as a blacksmith's apprentice. The pay was very little but it provided enough money for him to finish the house. He lived in the house the next two years, trying his hand at various odd jobs to make ends meet. He couldn't hold a job very long because of his arrogant disposition and hot temper. With no money and a mounting list of debts, he quickly lost all his friends and began drinking heavily. In hopes of escaping his bad reputation, he gave himself a new name, Edward.

Despite her mother's strong hatred for Edward Shue, Zona married him on October 20, 1896, only weeks after they had first met. Her friends were baffled by her choice for a mate. Shue had very little education or ambition; he couldn't hold a job for very long; his anger problems had begun to show, and he often drank to excess. Some speculated that Zona was drawn to his tall, muscular figure, dark hair, and brown eyes. Others thought she had become pregnant again and was marrying him "just to make things right."

Edward and Zona moved into a two-story frame house near Livesay's Mill, where Edward found work in James Crookshanks' blacksmith shop. By day, Zona cleaned and decorated the house while Shue worked in the blacksmith shop. By night, they enjoyed cuddling in front of the fireplace and discussing their plans for the future. Over time, Edward Shue earned the trust and respect of Zona's friends.

While working at the blacksmith shop on the afternoon of January 23, 1897, Shue was approached by 11-year-old Andrew Jones, who began asking questions about horseshoes. The boy's repeated questions and incessant chatter soon got on Shue's nerves, so he offered him a quarter to go and see if Zona needed help with gathering eggs or doing housework. Andrew graciously accepted Shue's offer and scampered away; he arrived at the house five minutes later.

Having knocked on the door several times without an answer, Andrew walked around the outside of the house and tapped on a window. There was no answer.

Thinking Zona had gone to see a neighbor and would return soon, he went back to the front door and let himself in. Zona and Shue knew him, so they wouldn't mind. As he walked though the living room, he heard the ceiling squeak as if someone was upstairs. He walked through the doorway leading into the hall and found Zona lying at the foot of the staircase with her feet together and one hand on her stomach.

Her eyes open, she appeared to be staring at him. He spoke but she didn't respond. She lay completely still and oblivious to her surroundings. Andrew walked over to the staircase, knelt down, and put his hand on her forehead. It was cold. He then felt her hand. It was cold. Aside from the gurgling sounds that came from her stomach when he shook her, Zona was completely silent.

Andrew rushed out the door and ran to the blacksmith shop, where he told Edward Shue about his grisly discovery. Shue rushed home and carried Zona's body upstairs to the bedroom, where he laid her out on the bed, bathed her, and dressed her in a high-neck dress. He placed a veil over her face.

It was rather unusual for someone to prepare their spouse's body for burial; friends of the deceased usually performed the task. Meanwhile, Andrew ran to get the local doctor and medical examiner, Dr. George Knapp.

Shue sat by his wife's corpse, nervously rubbing her head and crying profusely as Dr. Knapp began his examination. A minute later, Knapp looked at Shue and commented that Zona's neck looked bruised. When he turned back around to investigate further, Shue sprang up from his chair and began cursing him, insisting that no one would ever strangle his lovely wife. At that point, Dr. Knapp concluded his examination and left.

Several days later, despite having performed only a brief examination, Knapp listed "everlasting faint" as being the cause of Zona's death. He later changed her cause of death to "childbirth," although she wasn't believed to be pregnant when she died. Some accounts allege that Zona, who was very slender, appeared somewhat "large" at Christmas. Rumor also says that Knapp had treated her for female trouble only a month before her death.

Zona's funeral was held at her mother's house two days later. Edward Shue kept a constant vigil at the head of her coffin, sobbing profusely and cradling her head between a pillow and a roll of cloth. Several mourners commented that Zona's head and neck didn't look natural. Shue then tied a scarf around her neck and told everyone that it had been her favorite. Oddly, he wouldn't allow anyone to come near her coffin and pay their respects. When they tried, he would become angry and order them to step back.

Before Zona's body was taken to Soule Methodist Church for burial, her mother removed the sheet from inside the coffin and tried to return it to Shue. He refused. After the burial, she took the sheet home to wash. The water turned red when she dropped the sheet into the washing bucket; and after a few minutes, it turned pink. That, coupled with Edward Shue's aggressive behavior at Zona's funeral, was enough to convince Mrs. Heaster that he had murdered her daughter. She began praying every night, asking that Zona be returned from death and be allowed to explain how she died.

Four weeks after the funeral, severe chills awakened Mrs. Heaster late one night. Her entire body shaking, she glanced at the woodstove near her bed. The fire was roaring, but the air around her was bitterly cold; she could even see her breath. She got out of bed and checked the windows; no cold air was coming in. She crawled back into bed and pulled up the covers. Then suddenly, the bedroom began to light up. The woodstove was the only known source of light in the room, but the light she saw was much different. Her eyes watering because of the bright light, she blotted them with the cloth of her pillow. When she regained her focus, she saw Zona's life-like apparition standing at the foot of her bed.

Zona's broken and severely bruised neck had swelled considerably, and her face, now pale blue, had become puffy. She then spoke to Mrs. Heaster, giving her the full account of how Edward Shue had strangled her, broke her neck, and pushed her down the stairs to make her death look like an accident.

Shue had become angry with Zona because she didn't cook any meat for dinner one night. The next morning at breakfast, he complained about the biscuits being cold. After an intense, heated argument, Zona ran upstairs. Edward followed. Catching her at their bedroom door, he turned her around and began shaking her violently. Her head pounding against the door, she tried to kick him. He then choked her, snapped her neck, and threw her body down the stairs.

It took Zona's ghost four nights to relate the full account of her death. She appeared in the same fashion each night, talking for thirty minutes and then disappearing. After the ghost bade farewell, Mrs. Heaster wrote down everything she had been told. A week later, she visited John Alfred Preston, the local prosecutor, and asked him to file murder charges against Edward Shue. Preston didn't say whether he believed her ghost story, but he agreed to take the case. His first order of business would be to question Dr. Knapp.

Knapp explained that his examination had ended prematurely because of Shue's outburst when he commented about Zona's neck. Knapp, who had attended Zona's funeral, also told Preston about Shue becoming angry whenever someone came near her coffin.

Preston then executed the paperwork necessary to have Zona's body exhumed and autopsied. Shue objected fiercely upon learning of the impending autopsy; he insisted that his lovely wife be allowed to rest in peace. An article entitled, "Foul Play Suspected," appeared in the local newspaper a short time later.

In late February, Zona's body was exhumed and taken to a nearby schoolhouse for examination by Dr. Knapp and two other physicians. Five witnesses were present, including Edward Shue, who sat in a corner whittling a stick and complaining about his wife's privacy being violated. The autopsy report, issued in early March, stated that Zona's neck bore finger marks and was broken at the first joint, and that her windpipe had been crushed. The report also stated that undigested biscuits, butter, and raspberry jelly were found in her stomach, which supports the ghost's allegation that the crime took place right after breakfast. Authorities took Edward Shue into custody and charged him with murder.

A lynch mob formed outside the jail in nearby Lewisburg, demanding that Shue be released into their custody. Sherriff's deputies arrested and charged the mob's four leaders. While awaiting his trial, Shue continually boasted about the lack of evidence against him, insisting that the jury would acquit him. He also expressed his desire to marry four more women during his lifetime, boasting that he had always wanted seven wives.

Edward Shue's long-awaited trial began in late June of 1897 at the courthouse in Lewisburg. Many felt that Dr. Knapp's autopsy report would be sufficient to convict him, but the report was excluded from evidence at the last minute. Knapp, who was licensed to practice medicine, was not licensed to perform autopsies. Therefore, his autopsy report couldn't be used as evidence. The only evidence against Shue would be the testimony of Zona's ghost.

To stand a chance of winning the case, the state would need to call Mrs. Heaster to the witness stand and have her read aloud the notes she had made when Zona's ghost visited her. In addition, the jury would have to believe in ghosts. Shue's defense attorney, on the other hand, said that "hearsay from a ghost" would make a mockery of the American legal system, and would never be taken seriously by a jury. His plan was to diminish Mrs. Heaster's credibility by making her admit to fabricating her account of Zona's ghostly visits.

When Mrs. Heaster took the witness stand, Prosecutor Preston confined his questions to the basic facts in the case, carefully making sure not to mention her alleged encounters with Zona's ghost. During cross-examination, Shue's defense attorney asked her a long series of detailed questions about Zona's ghostly visits, sometimes asking the same question twice or more. His strategy was to trick her into contradicting herself, which would diminish her credibility as a witness.

Mrs. Heaster stuck to her story throughout the trial, insisting that she had been awake during the ghostly visits and that she fully understood everything the ghost had told her. Having run out of steam and wit, Shue's frustrated attorney rested his case.

After barely an hour of deliberation, the jury returned a guilty verdict against Edward Shue. In one of the oddest events in American legal history, the testimony of a ghost helped convict a man of murder. After being sentenced to life in prison, Edward Shue was transferred to the West Virginia State Penitentiary at Moundsville, where he died of typhoid fever in March of 1900.

Mary Heaster lived out a normal life, dying in 1916. Zona Heaster-Shue's ghost was never seen or heard from again. In the 1970's, Soule Methodist Church and the citizens of Greenbrier County replaced Zona's aging gravestone with a brand new one. The State of West Virginia placed a historical marker near the cemetery where Zona rests.

❦ FIFTEEN ❧

Moundsville Prison

*K*NOWN SIMPLY AS "MOUNDSVILLE," THE WEST VIRGINIA State Maximum Security Prison was built between 1866 and 1876. With its prominent stone walls and Gothic architecture, the imposing facility towers above the town of Moundsville, West Virginia.

The prison originally housed 450 of the state's most violent criminals. Due to skyrocketing crime rates in the Depression Era, the facility was housing more than 1,000 prisoners by the early 1930's. The massive influx of prisoners forced prison officials to assign three or more inmates to a single, five-by-seven cell. Expansion of the overcrowded facility was postponed for nearly thirty years. When the expansion finally occurred, Moundsville Prison was still overcrowded.

The prison's deadly combination of dangerous criminals, small cells, and deplorable living conditions made the facility a fertile breeding ground for serious trouble. Major riots broke out on two occasions, and inmates even murdered each other on occasion.

Many of Moundsville's inmates were hardened criminals serving life sentences; they had nothing to lose by misbehaving. Their guiding philosophy, "to kill or to be killed," landed Moundsville atop the U.S. Department of Justice's list of the country's most violent correctional facilities. In total, 36 murders were committed at Moundsville, and most of them were revenge killings.

In 1986, the West Virginia Supreme Court ruled that the facility's tiny cells constituted cruel and unusual punishment, and that Moundsville's environment didn't promote rehabilitation. As a result, the court ordered the prison shut down; Moundsville's last 700 prisoners left in 1995.

Moundsville also saw its share of executions. Eighty-five men were hanged there between 1899 and 1949. Up until June 19, 1931, the public was allowed to attend hangings at Moundsville Prison. On that date, an inmate named Frank Hyer was hanged for murdering his wife. He was decapitated instantly when the trap door opened and the noose bore his full weight. Those who witnessed the atrocity fled quickly, and the public was no longer allowed to attend hangings. Nine men died by electrocution at Moundsville between 1951 and 1965, when West Virginia abolished the death penalty. Paul Glenn, an inmate, built the prison's electric chair, "Old Sparky."

In addition to the many executions and homicides that occurred behind its massive walls, Moundsville's suicide rate was among the highest prison suicide rates in the country. The prison's many suicides would later play a role in making it one of the country's most haunted locations.

Also contributing to Moundsville's gloomy past were the harsh and atrocious methods of punishment administered by prison officials. As early as 1886, officials were caught hiding whips and other weapons from state inspectors. One prison official resigned from his post and told the press about the acts of torture being committed at Moundsville. He also described in meticulous detail the tools used by prison officials to torture inmates.

Invented at Moundsville, the "Kicking Jenny" was a curved, pedestal-like device that stood about four feet tall. The prisoner was stripped naked and forced to bend over the device, allowing his chest and stomach to rest along the curve. His hands were then stretched around the remaining curve and tied down with high-tension rope. The person assigned to whip the prisoner would take a heavy leather whip and beat him until he was almost dead.

Another tool, the "Shoo-Fly," was designed so that the prisoner could be placed with his feet in the stocks, his arms pinioned, and his head strapped. Once he was positioned correctly, someone would use a high-pressure hose to spray ice-cold water into his face. The procedure would continue until the prisoner had nearly strangled to death.

With its grim history of torture, murders, riots, suicides, and executions, the Moundsville Prison complex is a hotbed of paranormal activity. Phenomena such as apparitions, poltergeist activity, disembodied voices, residual hauntings, and unexplained cold chills are often experienced there. Where does one begin to describe such a wide range of paranormal activity in such a big place?

Just inside the main entrance is the Wheel House, a large, circular cage that revolved like a wheel and routed newly processed prisoners to appropriate areas. Operated by a guard, the cage also separated the warden and his family from the prisoners. Witnesses have seen the old cage rotate by itself, and have heard disembodied voices as it turned.

This phenomena is consistent with a residual haunting, whereby an event, usually tragic, replays itself continually. Because going through the gate signaled the official end to their freedom, new prisoners were usually overwhelmed by grief and anxiety when they entered the cage for the first time. The turning of the cage and the sound of disembodied voices could be psychic residue left behind by prisoners entering the facility for the first time.

The "Sugar Shack," a recreation area located in the prison's basement, was one of the facility's most dangerous areas. Used when weather conditions prevented use of the outdoor recreation area, the poorly guarded Sugar Shack saw its fair share of fighting, stabbings, and other atrocities. Witnesses occasionally report seeing apparitions of prisoners and guards roaming the area. There are also reports of nearby doors opening and closing by themselves.

The infamous prison's Protective Custody Yard was where rapists, child molesters, and "snitches" exercised and played outdoor sports. These prisoners were quarantined from the general prison population because of the crimes they had committed or because they had snitched on other inmates. Phenomena encountered in the Protective Custody Yard include strange odors, disembodied laughter, and an occasional thumping sound that fades quickly when people mention hearing it.

Prisoners aged 65 or older and in poor health were housed at the "Old Man Colony," where many natural-cause deaths occurred. When visiting this section of the prison, witnesses occasionally report seeing apparitions and feeling a strong sense of isolation and despair.

Moundsville's most dangerous inmates were housed in a two-level block of cells called, "The Alamo." Located in the prison's infamous North Hall, each cell in The Alamo housed only one prisoner. The prisoner was usually confined to his cell 24 hours a day. However, confinement didn't prevent The Alamo's prisoners from hurling urine and vomit at guards and other staff, or from making their own knives and killing each other when they were allowed to step out of their cells.

For years, The Alamo has been home to disembodied choking and groaning sounds. Very loud and clear, the grotesque sounds are often attributed to psychic residue left by despondent prisoners who hanged themselves. Along the same lines, people have reported feeling a gripping sensation around their necks while standing in some of The Alamo's cells. The same gripping sensation, coupled with feelings of emotional despair and uneasiness, has also been reported by visitors to "The Hole," an area of the prison's basement that was used for disciplining prisoners.

The oldest part of Moundsville Prison is the Wagon Gate, a small building that housed prisoners temporarily and served as the facility's execution chamber when hangings took place. Hangings occurred on the second floor, where the victim's body fell through a trap door in the floor. In addition to occasional choking sounds and sudden temperature drops, the Wagon Gate is reputed to harbor poltergeist activity such as knocks on the walls and floors.

Perhaps the most popular room at Moundsville is the electrocution chamber, which still houses the electric chair used to execute nine men over a fourteen-year period. Particular to the electrocution chamber, according to some witnesses, is the occasional smell of electrical wires burning and the faint aroma of meat burning. If such accounts are true, a residual haunting is taking place in the electrocution chamber.

Moundsville Prison also saw its share of celebrity inmates, whose crimes were so infamous that their names became household words. Moundsville's most infamous celebrity inmate was none other than Charles

Manson who, along with his family of followers, committed a series of brutal murders in California during the late 1960's. Manson, who is currently doing time in California for the murders, was an inmate at Moundsville several years before he moved to California. In 1983, Manson wrote to the Moundsville superintendent and requested to be returned to Moundsville so he could be near his relatives in West Virginia. His request was denied.

Another infamous criminal, one who didn't make it out alive, was Erasmus Stribbling Trout "Edward" Shue, the man who allegedly murdered his wife, Zona Heaster-Shue, in rural Greenbrier County, West Virginia. His conviction was based solely on the testimony of a ghost. Shue died at Moundsville in 1900 when he succumbed to a typhoid fever epidemic. He is buried in an unmarked grave nearby.

Thousands of men entered the West Virginia State Maximum Security Prison at Moundsville. While some eventually regained their freedom, many died from natural causes, suicide, murder, and execution. It should come as no surprise that the facility now abounds with paranormal activity. Paranormal investigators and television shows have visited the old prison on numerous occasions and verified the many shocking claims made by visitors. At the time of this writing, the facility is open for daylight tours and overnight paranormal excursions.

❧ SIXTEEN ❧

Woodlawn Plantation

S PRAWLING PLANTATIONS AND STATELY OLD MANSIONS dating back to the eighteenth century adorn northern Virginia's rolling landscape. Once home to Southern belles and gentlemen, the vast plantations with their elegant mansions are now home to caretakers, tourists, and in many cases, ghosts as well.

Each plantation has absorbed its share of happiness, hope, tragedy, and death over the years. Having stood witness to so many tragedies and oft-conflicting emotions, it should come as no surprise that these old plantations abound with ghostly activity. One such plantation is Woodlawn, located in Alexandria, Virginia.

Perched atop a breezy hill overlooking the Potomac River and George Washington's Mount Vernon estate, Woodlawn is nestled on 2,000 acres that George Washington gave to his stepdaughter, Nelly Custis, and her husband, Major Lawrence Lewis. Completed in 1805, Woodlawn's Federal-style mansion was designed by U.S. Capitol architect, Dr. William Thornton.

Like other old homes, Woodlawn's floors creak, its staircase rattles, and a cool breeze permeates the air when a closet is opened. The faces in the pictures on its walls follow you around the room. While each of those characteristics can be explained logically, other forces present at Woodlawn have defied logical explanation for years. Ghosts, usually spirits of former owners and servants, roam the house and grounds at all hours of the day and night.

Woodlawn's most notable ghost is that of George Washington. He is occasionally seen riding a white horse near the gardens, checking to make sure everything is being kept up.

Much of Woodlawn's ghostly activity centers on an old well located in the passageway that connects the kitchen with the main house. The safety lid covering the well's opening is usually propped open, but staff members must close it occasionally. Ghostly activity throughout the mansion increases three-fold when the lid is closed. On many occasions, staff members have shut and secured the safety lid at night, only to find it wide open the next morning. In some instances, the item used to secure the lid had been knocked to the floor.

Some paranormal researchers believe that houses built above wells are the most susceptible to hauntings because the wells connect to streams deep in the ground, which creates a conduit used by the spirit world to enter the house. If that theory holds water, one could assume that a well is a human-made vortex, or gateway, through which the spirit world passes into the material world. Assuming once again that the above theory is correct, why would ghostly activity increase, rather than decrease, when the well is capped?

The theory's proponents argue that the spirits become misguided or confused, perhaps even angry, when the well's safety lid prevents them from passing back to their world. The spirits then begin searching about the house for another passage into the spirit world. Other researchers disagree, saying that Woodlawn's spirits occupy specific areas and never leave.

Each area of Woodlawn seems to have its own spirit, and in most cases, the spirit represents someone who lived, worked, or died there. Woodlawn's most active area seems to be the upstairs bedrooms and hallway.

Thumping sounds are sometimes heard in the hallway late at night. The sounds are louder and more pronounced than footsteps, but the pace is eerily similar. Some believe the mysterious thumping is attributable to the ghost of a previous owner, John Mason, who had a wooden leg. Others believe the thumping comes from the ghost of Major Lawrence Lewis, who reportedly walked with a cane because of gout and severe arthritis.

Although the hallway ghost simply paces back and forth, the ghosts who occupy the adjacent rooms are more versatile. Witnesses standing outside the house have observed human-like figures moving around in the Lafayette bedroom window when no one was inside the house. In another case involving the Lafayette bedroom, a ghost allegedly tried to change a baby's diaper.

In the 1930's, a baby was left alone in a crib and soon began to cry. When her mother rushed into the bedroom to see what was wrong, she found the baby – her diaper soaked – lying atop a dresser across the room. Perhaps one of Woodlawn's ghosts had noticed that the infant needed her diaper changed.

The ghost of a house servant occasionally opens the door for people who enter the nearby Lorenzo bedroom. While the experience seems quite frightening, the ghost isn't believed to be dangerous. The same ghost may be responsible for the friendly tap on the shoulder that some overnight guests receive when they don't hear the alarm clock. The Lorenzo bedroom is also home to candles that sometimes light by themselves, right before dusk. Some have suggested that the house servant is readying the room for the evening.

Woodlawn's master bedroom is home to lights turning on and off by themselves and sudden gusts of chilly air. Visitors also report seeing apparitions of people dressed in period clothing. The apparitions, who usually stand near a window, last only five to ten seconds before disappearing.

Woodlawn, like so many other old plantations, has its fair share of ghosts. Whether they come from previous owners, an old well, or a mixture of both, we can't be sure; but regardless of their origin, Woodlawn's ghosts are the perfect example of Southern hospitality. They open doors for us; they entertain us from upstairs windows; they turn on the lights for us; they make sure we awaken when the alarm clock sounds, and they will even try to change a baby's diaper.

✌ SEVENTEEN ✣

The Cavalier Hotel

IRST OPENING ITS DOORS IN 1927, THE TRENDY Cavalier Hotel in Virginia Beach was among the most fashionable hotels on the East Coast. Catering to actors, politicians, and business moguls of the day, the classy hotel offered first-rate amenities and a stunning view of the Atlantic Ocean.

The Cavalier's guest list included the likes of Adolph Coors, Judy Garland, Will Rogers, F. Scott Fitzgerald, and Ginger Rogers. Well-known entertainers, such as Frank Sinatra, Glenn Miller, Tommy Dorsey, and Lawrence Welk, graced the stage at the hotel's world-famous Beach Club for over three decades. Ten U.S. presidents have stayed at the high-society institution or given speeches there, which earned it the nickname, "The Aristocrat of the Virginia Seashore."

The hotel's Hunt Room Grill, with its roaring fireplace and rustic ambiance, was a favorite of the upper echelon. 1930's and 40's big band sensation Glenn Miller frequented the grill when his world-renown orchestra performed at the Beach Club. Guests often spotted Miller in the Hunt Room before and after his legendary performances, sitting in a corner chair and sipping a martini. Even today, sixty-five years after he went missing over the English Channel, Miller still drops by on occasion.

Like the Hunt Room Grill, the Pocahontas Dining Room sees its share of ghostly activity as well. Guests often report the feeling of being watched, even when others aren't present. The dining room is also home to a waiter who walks though its walls as if they aren't there. To him, they don't exist. Perhaps he is trapped in an era such as the 1930's, when the dining room was laid out differently. If that's the case, he only sees the room as it appeared back then.

Tragedy wasted no time in striking the Cavalier. Two mysterious deaths occurred on the sixth floor within two years of its grand opening. It is rumored that the hotel's first owner, devastated by the infamous stock market crash of 1929, went to the sixth floor and took his life.

A mysterious man dressed in 1920s attire has been wandering the hallways of the sixth floor for years. Believed to be the hotel's first owner, he paces back and forth or stands near a window by the elevator. He also ventures downstairs on occasion to ring the check-in bell and throw papers onto the office floor.

In addition to the stock market crash, another great business tragedy occurred in the 1920's. The year 1920 marked the beginning of the Prohibition Era, when it was illegal to buy, sell, or consume alcoholic beverages anywhere in the United States (Author's note: Some individual states had enacted prohibition statutes much earlier). Although the country's business climate was healthy, manufacturers of alcoholic beverages were forced to explore alternatives. One such company was Adolf Coors and Company, one of the country's leading beer manufacturers.

The company was based in Denver, Colorado, where

state-sponsored prohibition had gone into effect in 1916. At that time, Adolf Coors converted his brewery to make malted milk. The company also manufactured porcelain and ceramic products made from clay mined in nearby Golden, Colorado.

By 1929, the company had made only a modest profit selling malted milk and ceramics, and most of Adolf Coors' fortune was invested in stocks. By June of that year, the U.S. economy was taking frequent nosedives, which triggered a massive sell-off in the stock market. The sell-off brought the value of stock down so low that the stock market crashed in October. Adolph Coors never lived to see that day, but the economic downturns earlier that year undoubtedly had a negative effect on his net worth.

Coors, like many business moguls who visited the East Coast, often stayed at the Cavalier Hotel. It was there, on June 5, 1929, that Coors plummeted to his death from a sixth floor window. It's unclear whether he committed suicide – which was entirely possible – or was pushed through the window. Shattered glass found on the ground below suggests the latter. Investigators said he could have easily opened the window and jumped had it been his intention.

Regardless of his cause of death, many believe that the spirit of Adolph Coors, who was 82 at the time of his death, still lingers at the Cavalier. Random cold spots on the sixth floor are attributed to his presence, as are frequent sightings of a well-dressed, older gentleman walking the hallways and front lobby. Some have even claimed to hear the thumping sound of a human body hitting the ground, next to the hotel.

The Cavalier's front desk occasionally receives calls from guests complaining about a cat scratching at their door. The hotel's staff repeatedly denies the existence of a resident cat. According to legend, a cat escaped from a guestroom one night and led its owner, a little girl, on a wild goose chase around the entire building. The chase ended when the cat jumped into the swimming pool. Seeing her beloved cat twisting and fighting to keep afloat, the little girl quickly removed her shoes and jumped into the pool to save him. Sadly, neither the little girl nor her cat survived. People have theorized that the mysterious cat roaming the halls is the ghost of the drowned cat, searching for his young owner.

There are also reports of an elderly African American gentleman who often stands on the staircase that leads to the sixth floor. Wearing a 1930's-era bellhop uniform and waving his hands in the air, he warns visitors not to proceed because there are ghosts on the sixth floor. When asked about the man, the hotel's staff insists that his description doesn't fit anyone who works there.

The Cavalier Hotel is ripe with many other ghostly phenomena. The piano downstairs occasionally plays by itself, and it's not uncommon for a toilet to flush by itself or a footstep to be heard where no one is walking. Dirty bathroom towels in guestrooms have been swapped for clean towels when no housekeepers were around.

The infamous but aristocratic Cavalier Hotel lives on, and you, too, can experience it. There are now two facilities: Cavalier on the Hill, which is the older, haunted building, and the Cavalier Oceanfront, which is a more modern building. Make sure to stay in the older building, and don't forget to request the sixth floor. Don't stand too close to the windows.

❧ EIGHTEEN ❧

The Gray Man

*I*T'S NO WONDER WHY SOUTH CAROLINA REPUTEDLY HAS more ghosts than any state in the Southeast. Every old plantation home seems to be haunted by a former owner; every lighthouse seems to be haunted by a former lightkeeper, and every old building seems to be haunted by someone who died there. Why are there so many ghosts in South Carolina?

Some say the often-violent deaths associated with being at sea is to blame, but that only explains a few hauntings in the coastal areas. Others believe that people with strong, dominant personalities often become ghosts when they die. That theory would certainly apply to South Carolina, seeing as how so many of its residents of long ago were wealthy plantation owners.

One of South Carolina's most famous tales is that of The Gray Man of Pawley's Island, a coastal community located in the Tidelands of Georgetown County. The Gray Man has roamed the beaches there for more than a hundred years. He's not what most people would call a *ghost*, but his manifestations and the meaning behind them are as intriguing and frightening as the spookiest ghostly encounters.

At four miles long and only a quarter mile wide at its widest point, Pawley's Island is especially susceptible to damage from hurricanes and tropical storms. Houses are either leveled by the wind or carried out to sea by raging waters; sand dunes are flattened, and entire families are swept away.

Hurricane Hazel swept the tiny island in 1954, destroying everything in its path: homes, restaurants, fishing piers, and trees. Miraculously, no fatalities resulted from Hazel because of a hurricane warning system. In addition to the hurricane warning systems put in place by the government, Pawley's Island has its own hurricane warning system. He is called, *The Gray Man.*

The Gray Man wanders the beaches during hurricane season, warning residents about impending hurricanes and tropical storms, and urging them to flee the island. Oblivious to his surroundings unless a hurricane or tropical storm is approaching, his Dick Tracy-like appearance frightens or startles those who encounter him. Sightings of The Gray Man are sporadic, and they usually occur well before the government's warning systems are triggered.

According to legend, those who encounter The Gray Man and heed his warning will be spared when the storm arrives. Their homes will be spared as well. Many who encounter The Gray Man admit their homes would no longer exist had they not heeded his warning.

Encounters with The Gray Man have been reported for more than a hundred years. He first appeared on Pawley's Island in 1822, to a young woman in the former resort town of North Inlet. She had no way of knowing who he was or what he wanted; she saw him one minute and he was gone the next minute. The next day, her father took their family to Charleston and a hurricane struck Pawley's Island. The two-day storm killed almost everyone in North Inlet and killed over 300 persons on the outlying islands of South Carolina and Georgia.

The Gray Man appeared again in 1893, silently warning a local family about an impending storm. They heeded his warning and they, along with their home, were spared. Known as the Sea Islands Hurricane, the powerful storm hit Pawley's Island in the early morning hours of August 28th. The 16-foot storm surge killed almost 1,500 people and destroyed nearly as many homes.

The Gray Man appeared twice in 1954, once in April before a tornado struck, and again in October, before Hurricane Hazel struck.

A young man and his new bride were enjoying their honeymoon on the island when they suddenly heard a knock at their door about 5 A.M. No one would be knocking at that time, especially during a honeymoon, unless there was an urgent matter needing attention.

At the door stood an older man wearing a wrinkled gray trench coat and a gray hat pulled down to his eyebrows. The man said the Red Cross wanted everyone to leave because a hurricane was approaching the area. The scenario seemed reasonable enough at first, but the man suddenly disappeared. He never even stepped off the porch.

The young couple hurried off the island. Hurricane Hazel, a Category 4 storm, struck the island a few hours later. It total, the storm killed almost 100 people and destroyed 15,000 homes along its path. The small honeymoon cottage was spared.

In September of 1989, a couple who lived on Pawley's Island was taking their morning walk along the beach when they spotted an older man who was dressed in gray. He gazed at them and began walking in their direction. Then suddenly, he vanished. Knowing what the Gray Man's appearance meant, the couple quickly packed their bags and left the island. Two days later, Hurricane Hugo, another Category 4 storm, struck the island. In total, Hugo killed 76 people and caused damage that totaled in the billions of dollars.

From whence did the Gray Man come? Why is he so intent on protecting the residents of Pawley's Island? There are as many theories to his existence and purpose as there are ghosts in South Carolina, and perhaps even more.

The most popular theory, dating back to the nineteenth century and based entirely on local legend, states that a young girl who lived on the island with her wealthy family became romantically involved with a man from Charleston. Her family didn't approve of him, so they tried to force him out of their daughter's life by persuading him to join the military and go overseas.

He took the girl's family up on their offer and sailed to Europe, much to the girl's chagrin. She waited months for her lover to return, but he didn't. Assuming he had met another woman while abroad, her family – perhaps to inflict more grief – told her that he had died while overseas. The young woman grieved her loss for nearly a year, during which time her parents introduced her to a wealthy young man from Charleston. Nature took its course and she eventually married him. They chose to live in a small house on her parents' property by the ocean.

One day, a terrible storm bore down on the Atlantic Ocean and made several ships capsize. The next day, two of the couple's slaves spotted what looked like debris on the beach near the house. They went to investigate. They found the shriveled and poorly nourished body of a man who had been thrown overboard when his ship capsized. He had managed to stay afloat by holding to a large piece of driftwood. The man could hardly speak.

The sun had burned his skin badly and sapped away most of his energy.

The slaves fetched a wooden board and a blanket, then carefully loaded the man onto the board, covered him with the blanket, and carried him into the house. Upon seeing the man, the young mistress of the house fainted. He was her long lost love from years past; he had never died in the first place. She awoke from her faint and told the slaves to remove him from the house and to care for him in their quarters. As he regained his strength over the next few days, he talked with the slaves and accidentally learned about his former lover's marriage.

Heartbroken and angry, the man bade farewell to the slaves and slowly made his way to the beach. He walked out into the ocean and he was never seen again. He became The Gray Man, and his mission is to protect the residents of Pawley's Island.

Regardless of what one chooses to believe, the saga of the mystical Gray Man of Pawley's Island, South Carolina is one of the most enduring and usual stories of its kind. Should you ever visit the South Carolina coast and see him, pack your belongings and leave; your vacation is over.

❧ NINETEEN ❧

The Battery

KNOWN FOR ITS EXQUISITE CHARM AND GRACIOUS hospitality, the city of Charleston, South Carolina is deeply rooted in history and Southern culture. Over the years, this historic coastal city has stood witness to pirate hangings, unsolved murders, bloody duels, and a four-year Civil War bombardment, making it one of the Southeast's most haunted cities.

In the early eighteenth century, Charleston was bursting at the seams with pirates, many of whom are now legendary. Charleston was where the notorious pirate, Blackbeard, kidnapped a prominent politician and his young son, releasing them only after authorities had met his demands for medical supplies. Charleston was also the place where female pirate Anne Bonny met her infamous pirate husband, James Bonny.

A wealthy Charleston gentleman named Stede Bonnet became a pirate in order to escape his wife's nagging. He used his money to build a pirate vessel he called, *The Revenge*. Known as "The Gentleman Pirate," Bonnet was captured and hanged in 1718, the same year in which the city tried and hanged nearly 50 pirates.

Pirates were hanged from oak trees at White Point, an area so named because sun-bleached piles of oyster shells covered its beaches. The oak trees still stand today, and many believe the pirates who once dangled from their branches now haunt the area. Witnesses have seen ghostly, pirate-looking figures wandering near the trees on occasion, and gagging sounds are sometimes heard in the area at night.

White Point later became known as, "The Battery." Situated at the confluence of the Ashley and Cooper Rivers, The Battery was home to Fort Broughton and Fort Wilkins during the early eighteenth century and later served as an artillery installation during the Civil War. With pirate hangings and Civil War conflicts in its past, The Battery is one of Charleston's most haunted sections. One of The Battery's most active sites is the historic Carriage House Bed and Breakfast, located only a stone's throw from the mighty oaks where pirates were once hanged.

Built in 1843, the Carriage House Bed and Breakfast is home to faces that appear in mirrors, shutters that open and close by themselves, disembodied footsteps that roam empty hallways, and a mist that occasionally forms above guests' beds. No one knows how many ghosts reside at the historic bed and breakfast, but most activity there revolves around two distinct and very prominent ghosts: a headless torso that frequents Room 8, and a young man who frequents Room 10.

Described as a large, broad-shouldered man seen only from his waist to his neck, the torso ghost wears a heavy overcoat and reportedly floats around the room in an upright position. Witnesses say he breathes heavily, even growling and grunting on occasion, but never speaks. With his disfigured appearance, the torso ghost terrifies even the bravest of people; but oddly enough, he is considered harmless.

The torso ghost's origin remains a mystery, but his grayish burlap overcoat leads some to believe he represents a Civil War soldier who was decapitated by an accidental munitions explosion. Others disagree, saying he more closely resembles a pirate.

The second ghost's appearance is far less frightening, but his behavior often makes up for it. Described as a well-dressed and immaculately groomed young man, he usually manifests as a shadow or the scent of fresh soap. Sometimes called "The Gentleman Ghost," he takes a liking to female guests by lying next to them and putting his arms around them. Although he displays incubus-like tendencies, he is quite the gentleman; he leaves if the woman resists his advances.

Some believe he's the spirit of a young man whose family owned the house many years ago, before it became a bed and breakfast. Legend says he was a college student who jumped to his death from an upstairs window.

Many restless spirits live in Charleston's Battery – many we've yet to identify, and many we've yet to encounter. They include hanged pirates, fallen Civil War soldiers, and Southern belles and gentlemen who once lived in The Battery's many old homes. If you are interested in history and ghosts, you owe it to yourself to visit Charleston and experience the Battery.

❧ TWENTY ❧

Sloss Furnace

IRMINGHAM, ALABAMA'S IRON PRODUCING LEGACY began in the early 1800's when the abundance of iron ore, limestone, and hardwood forests nearby made it an ideal place to produce iron. Birmingham became a major producer of iron in the years leading up to the Civil War; but unfortunately, the war wiped out most of the area's iron-production facilities.

The industry was slow to recover after the war because most hardwood forests in the area had already been cut down. In 1873, it was discovered that *coke*, a processed form of coal, could be used to make iron. That discovery, along with an abundant supply of coal, revived Birmingham's once-thriving iron industry.

Sloss Furnace dates back to 1881 when Colonel James Sloss built an iron processing facility in Birmingham. Sloss' first two furnaces were fired in 1882 and 1883, respectively, and his company grew over the next few years. In the 1890's, Sloss rebuilt the furnaces and added more processing equipment to the facility. By 1901, Sloss had retired and the company's name had become Sloss-Sheffield Steel and Iron Company.

Between 1927 and 1931, while most of the country suffered from the Great Depression, Sloss-Sheffield Steel and Iron Company replaced the original furnaces and automated much of their facility. The company's ownership changed two more times over the next four decades. Economic pressure forced the company to close in 1971. A National Historic Landmark, the old Sloss facility is now a museum.

There has always been an element of danger in working with iron. This was especially true in the nineteenth century when few safety regulations existed. Several men died working at Sloss Furnace, and the manner in which most of them died was quite gruesome. As one might expect, the old Sloss facility harbors ghosts. Most paranormal activity at Sloss centers on two prominent ghosts, both of whom represent people who suffered gruesome, tragic deaths at the facility.

The first ghost is the spirit of a young woman who died in the early 1900's. According to legend, she became pregnant out of wedlock and her friends, neighbors, and parents wanted nothing to do with her. Having become an outcast, she became depressed and decided to commit suicide. One day, she snuck into the facility and casually made her way to a hot furnace, where she climbed the ladder to the top. A supervisor began yelling for her to come down the ladder, but she ignored him. After closing her eyes and taking a deep breath, she jumped from the ladder and plummeted into a pool of red-hot, molten iron, which consumed her body instantly.

Not long after the incident, the company held an outdoor social event that included the likes of top executives and local politicians. As one of the executives was giving a speech, a white deer emerged out of nowhere and darted through the crowd, knocking over tables and making people spill their refreshments. No one noticed where the deer went after it wreaked havoc on the festive crowd, but several later said it had vanished. A day later, nearly everyone who had attended the event was attributing deer's presence to the young woman who had committed suicide.

The mysterious white deer reemerged at another

company event, three months later. Once again, it zipped through the crowd and made a big ruckus. The deer ended up attending every outdoor social event held at Sloss Furnace for the next forty years. Many people say the deer is a reincarnation of the young woman who jumped to her death in the molten iron.

The most prominent ghost at Sloss Furnace is Theophilus Jowers. An ironworker by choice, Jowers loved his job; he often remarked that furnaces were his home. He spent his formative years learning to make charcoal and prepare molds used to shape metal. He later became the Assistant Foundryman at Alice Furnace #1 in Birmingham, where he was responsible for making sure special projects were completed properly and on time. It wasn't uncommon for him to pitch in and help with a project.

One day in the fall of 1887, Jowers decided to help two men remove the bell from atop a tall furnace and replace it with a new one. While standing above the furnace and detaching the old bell from its frame, he lost his footing and plummeted into the molten steel below. His co-workers fished out his skull, hipbones, and part of a shoe.

Soon after his death, Jowers' co-workers began experiencing strange phenomena. Some complained of an unusually cold spot near the furnace where he died, and others claimed to see his ghost wandering about the hottest part of the furnace, which often reached temperatures in excess of 2,000 degrees Fahrenheit. Jowers continued to haunt Alice Furnace #1 until it closed in the early 1900's. He then haunted Alice Furnace #2, walking through the molten steel every day until the facility closed in 1927.

If this chapter is supposed to be about Sloss Furnace, why are we discussing a ghost who haunted another furnace? As you remember, Jowers loved his work; he even said furnaces were his home. Sloss was the only furnace left in Birmingham after Alice Furnace #2 shut down. A man of his word, Jowers then began haunting Sloss Furnace – and he's still there today.

In the late fall of 1927, Theophilus Jowers' son and grandson were riding across the viaduct next to Sloss Furnace when they decided to stop the car and look at the facility. They liked to watch the workers and see the molten metal trickle through the machinery. As soon as John Jowers stepped out of the car, he spotted a man pacing back and forth through a shower of sparks next to some molten metal. His son also saw the man. The man, who wore no protective gear, was walking so near the molten metal that he couldn't have been human.

John saw the ghost many times on future trips to the Sloss viaduct, as did his son. They concluded that the mysterious figure was none other than Theophilus Jowers, staying true to his word that furnaces were his home.

In recent years, visitors have experienced even more phenomena at Sloss Furnace. The most active part of the facility seems to be the Blowing Engine Building, which is the oldest structure on the property. If you leave an object at any location inside the building, it will sometimes be in a different location when you return. People have also heard screams in the building on several occasions. Described as being high in pitch but low in volume, the phantom screams are believed to come from the floor – or from beneath the floor – of the aged building. It's also easy to take pictures inside the building and see orbs, mist, and blurs in the final product.

Although no proven, *scientific* correlation exists between photographic anomalies and the paranormal, some believe that, in certain cases, the anomalies can indicate the presence of paranormal activity.

Visitors have also seen a mysterious, glowing figure standing on a catwalk. The apparition, human-like but void of any discernable human features, appears no longer than five minutes at a time before fading away. Many people think the figure is Theophilus Jowers, continuing to stand watch over his beloved furnace.

❧ TWENTY-ONE ❧

The LaLaurie Mansion

NEW ORLEANS IS A CITY OF CONTRASTING MEMORIES. Mardi Gras makes people smile, yet Hurricane Katrina made people cry. You can experience top-notch musical entertainment in the same building where hundreds once died an epidemic. You can live in a house and be happy, yet many years ago, dozens of servants were tortured and mutilated in the very same house.

One of the most gruesome memories in the Crescent City's tragic history came at the hands of a wealthy mistress and her physician husband. The couple tortured and mutilated their servants, harvesting their still-alive body parts and using them for grotesque medical experiments. Doctor and Madame Delphine LaLaurie's cruel and sinister acts shocked the New Orleans community and left behind a horrific spiritual residue that will forever linger in the little shop of horrors known as, The LaLaurie Mansion.

Madame Delphine LaLaurie was born Marie Delphine Macarty in 1775. Her parents, Louis Macarty and Marie Jeanne Lovable, were prominent members of New

Orleans' elite, high society crowd. They were later killed in a slave revolt on the island of Haiti.

Delphine Macarty was married twice between 1800 and 1824. Both her husbands – one a Consul General for Spain, and the other a banker – died young and left her to care for their children. Her cousin, Augustin de Macarty, was mayor of New Orleans from 1815 until 1820, which undoubtedly helped her rise to prominence.

On June 25, 1825, she married Dr. Leonard Louis LaLaurie, a prominent local physician. Dr. LaLaurie was one of the area's only surgeons, and his peers considered him an expert in his field. In 1831, Dr. and Madame LaLaurie purchased a French Empire-style mansion at 1140 Rue Royale in the French Quarter.

Within days, expensive furniture, ornate mirrors, and elaborate paintings began arriving at what would become one of the city's most lavish mansions. Madame Delphine LaLaurie herself was quite fashionable with her long dark hair, blue eyes, and charming personality. She dressed in meticulous detail, always wearing the finest of dresses. Dr. LaLaurie was wealthy, handsome, and charming.

Dr. and Madame LaLaurie's lavish parties were the place to be seen in New Orleans; everyone who was anyone graced the mansion with their presence. Socially, the early 1830's were very productive for the wealthy couple. Their lavish lifestyle, numerous parties, and influential friends accelerated their rise to prominence.

Although life was going well for Dr. and Madame LaLaurie, many guests couldn't help but notice how nervous the servants became when Madame LaLaurie snapped her fingers or called out for them. They became even more nervous when they had to answer her questions or bring her something. Guests also noticed the harshness with which she spoke to the servants; her tone was very controlling and her orders usually included threats. Not wishing to jeopardize their relationship with one of New Orleans' most prominent and influential couples, the guests never broached the subject with Doctor or Madame LaLaurie.

Late one afternoon, Madame LaLaurie summoned a young female servant to her bedroom to brush her hair. Despite her brushing Madame LaLaurie's hair ever so gently, the young servant's brush hit a snag and Madame LaLaurie sprang from her chair in a fit of rage and began cursing the girl.

Terrified, the girl bolted out of the room and ran down the stairs. Madame LaLaurie, brandishing a leather whip, followed closely behind her. She ran through the courtyard, and then darted back inside the house and up the stairs. She then fled to the roof, where she hoped to find sanctuary. It did her no good, for Madame LaLaurie soon appeared and cornered her at the roof's edge. In the blink of an eye, the desperate servant girl turned around and jumped from the roof. She landed on the stone path in the courtyard.

Barely conscious and struggling to breathe, the girl was carried inside the mansion. She died minutes later. That night, Dr. and Madame LaLaurie took her body back to the courtyard and dumped it into an old well. A neighbor had witnessed much of the ordeal, including the girl's fatal jump and subsequent "burial."

At the time, New Orleans had an ordinance that outlawed the cruel treatment of servants. The neighbor filed a complaint against Dr. and Madame LaLaurie. Their close friend, Judge Caponage, addressed the complaint. Surprisingly, he ruled against Dr. and Madame LaLaurie, ordering them to pay a $300 fine and surrender all of their servants. Not to be outdone, Madame LaLaurie talked some of her relatives into buying the servants back for her.

Things were much different at the LaLaurie Mansion after the incident. Fewer parties were being thrown and fewer people were attending them. Having lost many patients because of the highly publicized ordeal, Dr. LaLaurie was forced to give up his medical practice and work in the field of anatomical research. Despite all the negative publicity they had received, the couple continued treating their servants viciously.

On April 10, 1834, a cook set the mansion on fire in hopes of drawing the public's attention to the many atrocities still being committed there. Firefighters carrying buckets of water and townspeople carrying boxes and blankets rushed to the mansion. The firefighters worked to contain the blaze as the townspeople, under the direction of Madame LaLaurie, moved her furniture outside and packed her belongings for her.

Having not seen any servants inside or outside of the mansion, which was very unusual, the townspeople asked Madame LaLaurie about the welfare and whereabouts of her servants. Her quick, simple answer was, "They all went somewhere down the street." Everyone knew better; her servants' well-being was the farthest thing from her mind.

The firefighters continued working until the blaze subsided and the smoke cleared. While combing the mansion for smaller, secondary fires and other hazards, the firefighters discovered the elderly cook who had started the fire. Gasping for breath and chained to a large wooden post in the kitchen, the cook told the firefighters that the other servants were in the attic. She explained that the "attic" was the mansion's most feared room; servants who were taken there never returned.

A concerned firefighter rushed through the house and found Madame LaLaurie standing on the front patio. He demanded the key to the attic, but she refused, saying there was no reason for them to enter the attic because the fire had been put out. Their curiosity aroused, several townspeople and firefighters ran inside the mansion, rushed up the stairs, and charged through the attic door, breaking it into several pieces. The attic was completely dark. They smelled the strong odor of human waste and several odors they couldn't identify. The men found candles in the adjacent hallway to help them see.

Entering the attic, they discovered three servants lying on their backs and chained to the floor by their hands and feet. Still alive, the servants' fully naked bodies were covered with honey; hundreds of tiny ants were crawling all over them. Another servant was chained to a nearby chair. Barely alive, a hole had been drilled through the top of his skull and a stick had been inserted in the hole. Firefighters tried speaking to him, but he wasn't of the mind to talk.

Moving farther into the attic, the firefighters discovered two dead servants hanging from the ceiling. Their entrails had been removed, and their necks had begun to decompose where the nooses where attached. Two others servants, unharmed but fully naked, were living together in a locked cage.

Ten more servants, some dead, were chained to the walls. Some had had their bones broken and reset at grotesque angles. Others had had limbs and other body parts removed or altered. In one case, and probably the first operation of its kind in America, certain body parts had been switched between a male servant and a female servant. Both were still alive.

It took little guesswork to determine what had been happening at the LaLaurie Mansion between 1832 and 1834. Dr. and Madame LaLaurie had devised an ingenious way to keep things running smoothly at the mansion while furthering Dr. LaLaurie's career as an anatomical researcher. Servants who angered Madame

LaLaurie were sent to the attic and tortured mercilessly. When the torture ceased, they became subjects of Dr. LaLaurie's bizarre medical experiments. Servants who were lucky enough not to experience the attic were never aware of what was happening; they only knew that no one ever returned from there.

A mob gathered outside the LaLaurie Mansion the next morning and demanded justice. Dr. LaLaurie's whereabouts were unknown, and Madame LaLaurie stayed inside the mansion. Legal authorities were nowhere to be found, and the angry mob grew larger by the hour. Later in the day, a horse-drawn carriage rolled up to the mansion's front steps and waited for Madame LaLaurie; it was time for her daily ride through the city. Dressed fashionably as ever, she walked out the door and boarded the carriage hurriedly.

The carriage quickly picked up speed as it rolled away from the mansion. Realizing that Madame LaLaurie was attempting to flee the city, the mob shouted obscenities at her as they began chasing the carriage and pelting it with cobblestones. The horses proved to be no match for the angry mob, however; Madame LaLaurie's carriage turned a corner and was gone forever.

She was taken to Bayou St. John, where she reportedly paid the captain of a schooner to carry her across Lake Pontchartrain to the town of Mandeville, Louisiana. Dr. LaLaurie, along with Delphine's two daughters, met her at Mandeville a week later and executed a power-of-attorney authorizing their relatives to handle their business affairs in New Orleans. They left Mandeville and went to Mobile, Alabama, where they boarded a ship for France. They lived out their lives peacefully in Paris, France. Rumor has it that Madame LaLaurie was killed by a wild boar in a hunting accident.

An old, weathered copper plate found in New Orleans' St. Louis Cemetery #1 in 1941 suggests that Madame

Delphine LaLaurie died on December 7, 1842, and that her body was returned to New Orleans secretly and entombed in an above-ground vault. The plate was not affixed to a vault when it was found; therefore, the exact location of her burial isn't generally known.

The vacant mansion was renovated over a thirty-year period. Stories of unusual noises, candles blowing out by themselves, and other anomalies weren't uncommon after the renovation. Two different tenants left the mansion after having lived there less than three months.

By 1920, the mansion had been renovated again and was being used as apartments. In one case, a man was awakened late at night by two cold hands pressing against his neck and throat. The hands began choking him when he tried to move his head. Another figure suddenly appeared and wrestled his assailant's hands away from his throat. The two servants then faded away. The man later described his assailant as a servant dressed in 1800's-period clothing.

The mansion became a furniture store in later years. The owner closed it down after his furniture inventory was destroyed on several occasions and without explanation. Madame LaLaurie apparently didn't care much for his furniture.

In the 1980's, the mansion was owned by two prominent local physicians. Their guests often reported hearing footsteps coming from the attic stairway, as well as disembodied voices coming from the guest bedrooms. Guests also reported hearing the sound of children laughing and playing in the courtyard; no children were present when the sounds were heard.

Another area of interest is the downstairs room with a restored fireplace. When workers were dismantling the old fireplace during a renovation project, they discovered a rolled-up charcoal drawing of Madame Delphine LaLaurie. Following the bizarre discovery, strange activity began to occur in the room. Tools went missing every day; mist occasionally came down the fireplace, and visitors often complained about their clothes being pulled by an unseen force.

The ghost of Madame LaLaurie haunts the mansion regularly. Over the years, many visitors have seen her and her disfigured servants wandering about the mansion's upstairs area. People have also spotted her ghost strolling around the mansion's balconies late at night. The quiet, pale figure seems oblivious to onlookers at first, but she suddenly disappears when people speak to her. Some claim to have actually talked with her.

A ghost believed to be Dr. Louis LaLaurie haunts an upstairs room that was used for storage when he lived there. Described as well dressed and having a meticulously groomed mustache, he stands quietly and observes guests from a distance. The smell of cigar smoke that occasionally fills the room is also associated with Dr. LaLaurie's ghost.

Perhaps the most astonishing event that has occurred at the LaLaurie Mansion in recent years was the discovery of several shallow graves beneath its old cypress floors. A previous owner has insisted that the house was built on top of an old Spanish graveyard, but tests proved that the bones found under the floor had been buried in the 1800's. In addition, the graves were too shallow and they were situated in too irregular of a pattern to have been part of a graveyard.

Although the bodies had decomposed, small amounts of hair were found near some of the skulls. The hair turned out to be from African Americans, which has fueled speculation that those buried beneath the old floor were Dr. and Madame LaLaurie's servants.

The number of servants tortured and murdered by Dr. and Madame LaLaurie remains a mystery. Taking into account the number of servants found in the attic when the mansion caught fire, as well as the number of human skeletons found beneath the floor in recent years, rest assured that their spirits will linger forever in Madame LaLaurie's little shop of horrors, known as the LaLaurie Mansion.

❧ TWENTY-TWO ❧

The Haunted Lighthouse at St. Augustine

FOUNDED BY THE SPANISH IN 1565, ST. AUGUSTINE, Florida is the oldest continuously occupied city in the continental United States. Like many of America's older cities, St. Augustine has seen its share of tragedy. Pirates raided the city in 1668; devastating yellow fever epidemics swept the city in 1821 and 1885; it became a battleground during the Seminole War of 1836, and it has endured many fires and hurricanes. Having witnessed so much tragedy over the centuries, St. Augustine is one America's most haunted cities.

Situated on the north end of Anastasia Island and rising 165 feet above sea level is the St. Augustine Lighthouse. Built between 1871 and 1874 to replace another lighthouse, many consider the current lighthouse to be the city's most haunted landmark. Seven people have died at the lighthouse, on the grounds, or in the ocean nearby: three lightkeepers, three children, and a lightkeeper's wife.

The first death occurred in 1853 when John Carrera,

a lightkeeper, died in the original lighthouse. Carrera's ghost hasn't been spotted, and for good reason. The original lighthouse, which was located a half-mile from the current structure, plummeted into the Atlantic Ocean when the shoreline eroded from around it. The next death occurred in 1859 when lightkeeper Joseph Andreu fell to his death while working atop the original lighthouse. Unlike Carrera's ghost, who is presumably at the bottom of the ocean, Andreu's ghost went ashore.

Lightkeepers have heard footsteps following them while making their rounds, and they believe Andreu is the culprit because the footsteps sound like the heavy boots worn by lightkeepers in the 1800's. How could relatively modern lightkeepers identify the clonking sounds made by 1800's-era work boots? In the 1940's, a pair of such boots was found in a storage room at the lightkeeper's residence. As a test, the lightkeeper wore the boots as he went about his routine for the next two days. Having heard the mysterious footsteps behind him on two previous occasions, he said they sounded identical to his own footsteps while wearing the old boots. The phantom footsteps are heard inside the lighthouse, in the gravel outside the lighthouse, and even in the lightkeeper's residence.

In April of 1889, a lightkeeper named William Harn died of tuberculosis while employed at the current lighthouse. Harn's ghostly apparition, described as a large male figure, frequents the cisterns in the basement of the lightkeeper's residence. On many occasions, visitors have smelled the distinct smell of cigar smoke in and around the lighthouse, as well as in the basement of the lightkeeper's residence. Harn is believed to be the culprit because he was reportedly a cigar smoker.

In September of 1894, a lightkeeper's wife died on the grounds near the lighthouse. The cause of her death unknown, her ghost often stands on the lighthouse's interior stairway and watches visitors on the ground floor. She has also been spotted walking in the yard outside the lighthouse.

The most tragic event in the lighthouse's history occurred when three young girls drowned in the Atlantic Ocean nearby. During the lighthouse's construction, a makeshift railway ran between the construction site and the ocean. A hand-powered railcar carried materials and trash between the construction site and the beach. The superintendent of construction, Hezekiah Pittee, had temporarily moved his family from Maine to Florida because the lighthouse would take four years to complete. Pittee's five children liked to ride the railcar for fun.

On July 10, 1873, the railcar derailed and plunged into the ocean with five children aboard. Workers managed to save a boy and a girl, but two of Pittee's daughters and the daughter of a construction worker weren't so fortunate.

Mary and Eliza Pittee are sometimes heard laughing in the lighthouse's tower late at night. Witnesses have also reported seeing the figures of two little girls standing on the lighthouse catwalk. Mary, who was 15 at the time of her death, reportedly wears the same blue dress she wore when she died. The playful ghost of a younger girl, presumed to be Eliza Pittee, frequents the lightkeeper's residence.

The ghosts we have discussed aren't the only supernatural entities lurking in the St. Augustine Lighthouse and the nearby lightkeeper's house. Workers and visitors have seen moving shadows inside and outside of the lighthouse, and disembodied voices have been heard in the lightkeeper's house. Tour guides have heard footsteps on the tower steps but found no one standing on them.

The St. Augustine Lighthouse and Museum, Inc. now

owns and maintains the historic lighthouse, which still functions as an official aid to navigation. It is open to the public for tours, and evening ghost tours are offered on occasion.

✍ APPENDIX ✍

*T*HE RESOURCE TABLES ON THE FOLLOWING PAGES contain driving directions and web addresses related to the stories in this book.

Every well-known legend, folktale, and ghost story has many different – and often conflicting – versions. Read the different web resources and decide which version you like the best. The web sites appear as a courtesy, and their being listed doesn't imply an endorsement. Each web address was functional at the time of publication.

Driving directions are provided for those wanting to see the locations mentioned in this book. The author wishes to make it clear that entering any location without proper permission is illegal, and that he does not promote, encourage, or condone any type of illegal activity.

Furthermore, some of the locations may be unsafe. It's best to assume that all haunted locations are unsafe unless you're told differently. Even if a location is deemed "safe," stay away from it if any *potential* safety issues exist. However, should you choose to continue – and get your leg broken, your eyeball punctured, or your neck snapped in two like a pretzel – it is of *your* own doing, and not mine. Remember, I am just here to entertain you with stories. Visiting allegedly haunted locations can be fun, but make sure you do it legally and safely.

~ ALABAMA ~
Sloss Furnaces

Web Sites

http://en.wikipedia.org/wiki/Sloss_Furnaces

http://facstaff.uwa.edu/ab/sloss.htm

http://www.frightfurnace.com/main.asp

Getting There

Sloss Furnaces National Historic Landmark
Twenty 32nd Street North
Birmingham, AL 35222
Phone: (205) 324-1911

~ ALABAMA ~
Cedarhurst Mansion

Web Sites

http://www.realhaunts.com/united-states/sally-carter/

http://facstaff.uwa.edu/ab/Cedarhurst htm

http://www.unsolvedmysteries.com/usm42048.html

Getting There

Cedarhurst is now a gated community at the corner of
Whitehurst and Northampton.

~ ARKANSAS ~
Mayhem on the Mississippi

Web Sites

http://en.wikipedia.org/wiki/Sultana_(steamboat)

http://sultanadisaster.com

http://genealogytrails.com/main/events/sultana.html

Getting There

The remains of the Sultana rest 20+ feet beneath a soybean field in Critenden County, Arkansas, near the town of Marion. A historical marker is nearby.

~ FLORIDA ~
The Haunted Lighthouse at St. Augustine

Web Sites

http://www.staugustinelighthouse.com

http://en.wikipedia.org/wiki/St._Augustine_Light

http://www.lighthousefriends.com/light.asp?ID=347

Getting There

The St. Augustine Lighthouse is located at 81 Lighthouse Avenue, Saint Augustine, FL.

~ GEORGIA ~
Savannah's Waving Girl

Web Sites

http://en.wikipedia.org/wiki/Florence_Martus

http://www.waymarking.com/waymarks/WM2EKW

http://www.elinordewire.com/wavinggirl.htm

Getting There

The "Waving Girl" statue is located in Morrell Park on East River Street, along Savannah's historic riverfront.

~ GEORGIA ~
The Curse of Lorenzo Dow

Web Sites

http://www.ghosttowns.com/states/ga/jacksonboro.html

http://en.wikipedia.org/wiki/Lorenzo_Dow

http://www.curbstone.org/index.cfm?webpage=56

Getting There

The Jacksonboro State Historical Marker is located on US 301 just south of the GA 24 intersection, 5 miles north of Sylvania, GA. The Seaborn Goodall house is nearby.

~ KENTUCKY ~
Waverly Hills TB Sanatorium

Web Sites

http://www.therealwaverlyhills.com/

http://en.wikipedia.org/wiki/Waverly_Hills_Sanatorium

http://www.abandonedonline.net/index.php?catid=84

Getting There

Waverly Hills is located off East Pages Lane, on a hill above the Bobby Nichols Golf Course. Waverly Hills Historical Society, Inc., (502) 933-2142.

~ LOUISIANA ~
Voodo on the Bayou (Marie Laveau)

Web Sites

http://en.wikipedia.org/wiki/Marie_Laveau

http://www.wendymae.com/voodoo/marie_laveau.html

http://www.controverscial.com/Marie%20Laveau.htm

Getting There

St. Louis Cemetery #1 is just off Basin Street, near the French Quarter in New Orleans. It is in a high-crime area; only visit with an organized tour group.

~ LOUISIANA ~
The LaLaurie Mansion

Web Sites

http://en.wikipedia.org/wiki/Delphine_LaLaurie

www.prairieghosts.com/lalaurie.html

www.unsolvedmysteries.com/usm383823.html

Getting There

The LaLaurie Mansion is located at 1140 Royal Street, in New Orleans' French Quarter. At the time of publication, the mansion is not accessible by the public.

~ MISSISSIPPI ~
The McRaven House

Web Sites

http://www.mcraventourhome.com/

http://en.wikipedia.org/wiki/McRaven_House

http://www.citizendia.org/McRaven_House

Getting There

The McRaven House
1445 Harrison St.
Vicksburg, MS 39180

~ NORTH CAROLINA ~
The Brown Mountain Lights

Web Sites

http://www.ibiblio.org/ghosts/bmtn.html

http://www.westernncattractions.com/BMLights.htm

http://farshores.org/pbmlight.htm

Getting There

The Brown Mountain Overlook is located 20 miles north of Morganton on NC highway 181, 1 mile south of the Barkhouse Picnic Area.

~ NORTH CAROLINA ~
The Devil's Tramping Ground

Web Sites

http://deviljazz.tripod.com/

http://wikipedia.org/wiki/Devil%27s_Tramping_Grounds

http://www.roadsideamerica.com/tip/3402

Getting There

The Devil's Tramping Ground is located on Devil's Tramping Ground Road in the Harper's Crossroads community, near Bennett, North Carolina.

~ SOUTH CAROLINA ~
The Gray Man

Web Sites

http://en.wikipedia.org/wiki/Pawley%27s_Island

http://www.suite101.com/article.cfm/folklore/50438

http://www.ghostsofearth.com/gray-man.html

Getting There

Pawley's Island, South Carolina is located 70 miles north of Charleston and 25 miles south of Myrtle Beach

~ SOUTH CAROLINA ~
The Battery

Web Sites

http://en.wikipedia.org/wiki/Battery_Park_(Charleston)

http://www.batterycarriagehouse.com/

http://www.realhaunts.com/united-states/the-battery/

Getting There

The Carriage House Inn is located at 20 S. Battery Street in Charleston, South Carolina. The phone number is (800) 775-5575.

~ TENNESSEE ~
The Bell Witch

Web Sites

http://www.bellwitch.org/

http://www.myspace.com/the_bell_witch

http://the-bell-witch.blogspot.com

Getting There

The Adams Museum and Archives
Highway 41
Adams, TN 37010

~ TENNESSEE ~
The Headless Conductor

Web Sites

http://midnite-walkers.com/haunted-tennessee.php

http://www.bellwitch.org/chapel.htm

http://www.answers.com/topic/chapel-hill-tennessee

Getting There

The crossing is on Feedmill Road in Chapel Hill, TN. The police patrol the area constantly, and they don't allow parking near the tracks.

~ TENNESSEE ~
The Nolichucky River

Web Sites

http://members.tripod.com/jayboy74/story29.html

http://en.wikipedia.org/wiki/Nolichucky_River

http://www.unclejohnnys.net/Rafting.html

Getting There

The Nolichucky River runs all through western North Carolina and eastern Tennessee. Unicoi County, Tennessee seems to be the most active, paranormally.

~ TENNESSEE ~
Mary at the Orpheum

Web Sites

http://wikipedia.org/wiki/Orpheum_theatre_(Memphis)

http://www.orpheum-memphis.com

http://cinematreasures.org/theater/1679

Getting There

The Orpheum Theatre is located at 203 South Main Street in Memphis, TN. The trolley still runs by there.

~ TEXAS ~
The Bragg Ghost Light

Web Sites

http://www.bigthicketdirectory.com/ghostroad.html

http://www.ghosts.org/ghostlights/bragg.html

http://release-me.net/story22.php

Getting There

Approx. 16 mi. west of Kountze, TX. The dirt road runs north-south starting at a bend on Farm-to-Market Road 787, which is 1.7 miles north of the intersection of FM 787-770, near Saratoga.

~ VIRGINIA ~
The Cavalier Hotel

Web Sites

http://www.cavalierhotel.com/

http://www.scaryforkids.com/cavalier-hotel/

http://www.historiesandhaunts.com/photos.htm

Getting There

The Cavalier Hotel is located at Oceanfront and 42nd Street in Virginia Beach, Virginia. Their telephone number is (800) 446-8199.

~ WEST VIRGINIA ~
The Greenbrier Ghost

Web Sites

http://en.wikipedia.org/wiki/Greenbrier_Ghost

http://www.wvculture.org/history/notewv/ghost1.html

http://www.roadsideamerica.com/story/11917

Getting There

The Greenbrier Ghost Historical Marker is located on US Highway 60 at Sam Black Church, West Virginia. Take I-64 until exit 156; sign is on south side of the bridge along US-60, west of Lewisburg.

~ WEST VIRGINIA ~
Moundsville Prison

Web Sites

http://www.roadsideamerica.com/story/10871

http://www.wvpentours.com/

http://crime.about.com/od/prison/a/moundsville.htm

Getting There

The building is located at the corner of 8th St. and Jefferson Ave. 818 Jefferson Ave., Moundsville, WV. (304) 845-6200

✍ BIBLIOGRAPHY ✍

Abernethy, Francis, ed. *Tales from the Big Thicket*. Denton: Univ. of North Texas Press, 2002.

Berry, Chester, ed. *Loss of the Sultana and Reminiscences of Survivors*. Knoxville: Univ. of Tennessee Press, 2005.

Brown, Alan. *Ghost Hunters of the South*. Univ. Press of Mississippi, 2006.

Brown, Alan. *Haunted Places in the American South*. Univ. Press of Mississippi, 2002.

"The Chapel Hill Ghost." *The Louisville and Nashville Railroad Employees' Magazine*, 1961, Vol. 37.

Chewning, Alpheus J. *Haunted Virginia Beach*. History Press, 2006.

Clauson-Wicker, Su. *West Virginia Off the Beaten Path, 6th (Off the Beaten Path Series)*. Guilford: Globe Pequot, 2006.

Deitz, Dennis. *The Greenbrier Ghost*. Mountain Memories, 1990.

DeWire, Elinor. "Savannah's Waving Girl." *Lighthouse Digest*, Feb. 1996.

Dow, Lorenzo. *The Stranger in Charleston, or the Trial and Confession of Lorenzo Dow*. 1822.

Fitzhugh, Pat. *The Bell Witch: The Full Account*. 2nd ed. Nashville: The Armand Press, 2003.

Floyd, Randall. *In the Realm of Ghosts and Hauntings*. New York: Harbor House, 2002.

Harden, John. *The Devil's Tramping Ground and Other North Carolina Mystery Stories*. Chapel Hill: The Univ. of North Carolina Press, 1980.

Jacobs, Claude F., and Andrew J. Kaslow. *The Spiritual Churches of New Orleans: Origins, Beliefs, and Rituals of an African-American Religion*. Knoxville: Univ. of Tennessee Press, 2001.

Johnson, Frank Roy. *Witches and Demons in History and Folklore*. Johnson, 1969.

Lewis, David W. *Sloss Furnaces and the rise of the Birmingham district: an industrial epic*. Tuscaloosa: Univ. of Alabama Press, 1994.

Lively, Lester N. "Can the Dead Return From the Grave?" *The Monroe Watchman* 16 Dec. 1971.

Louge, Rev. Frank. Sermon: *Shaking off the Dust*. The King of Peace Episcopal Church. <http://www.kingofpeace.org/sermon-070801.htm>.

Lyle, Katie Letcher. *The Man Who Wanted Seven Wives*. Chapel Hill, N.C: Algonquin Books of Chapel Hill, 1986.

McDonald, Archie P. "The Big Thicket Light." *All Things Historical* [Syndicated Column] 29 Jan. 2007.

McElhaney, Judy. *Ghost Stories of Woodlawn Plantation*. McLean: EPM Publications, 1992.

NcNeil, W. K. *Ghost Stories from the American South (American Storytelling)*. August House, 1989.

Nickell, Joe. "Voodoo in New Orleans." *The Skeptical Enquirer*, 2006.

Norman, Michael, and Beth Scott. *Haunted America*. New York: Tor Books, 2006.

Philips, David E. *Legendary Connecticut*. Willimantic, CT: Curbstone Press, distributed by InBook, 1992.

Potter, Jerry O. *The Sultana Tragedy: America's Greatest Maritime Disaster*. Pelican, 1992.

Price, Charles Edwin. *More Haunted Tennessee*. Overmountain Press, 1999.

Rhyne, Nancy. *Coastal Ghosts and Haunted Places from Wilmington, North Carolina to Savannah, Georgia*. Orangeburg, S.C: Sandlapper, 1989.

Roberts, Nancy. *Haunted Houses: Chilling Tales from Twenty-Four American Homes*. Old Saybrook, Conn: Globe Pequot Press, 1998.

Servis, Jr., Richard. "The Waving Girl." <http://richardservis.tripod.com>.

Sceurman, Mark, and Mark Moran. *Weird Georgia*. New York: Sterling, 2006.

"Sloss Blast Furnaces." *National Historic Landmark Listing*. National Parks Service.

Spencer, Susan. "Ghosts for Guests." *48 Hours*. CBS News, 2000.

Tallant, Robert. *Voodoo in New Orleans*. Gretna, La: Pelican, 1983.

Taylor, L. B. *Ghosts of Virginia*. Williamsburg: L.B. Taylor, 1993.

Taylor, Troy. *Haunted New Orleans Ghosts and Hauntings of the Crescent City*. Whitechapel Productions, 2000.

Taylor, Troy. *No Rest for the Wicked - History & Hauntings of American Crime & Unsolved Mysteries*. Whitechapel Productions, 2001.

Webb, Julie. "Louisiana Voodoo and Superstitions related to Health." *Assoc. of Schools of Public Health*, 1971. Abstract.

Wilson, Patty A. *Haunted West Virginia Ghosts and Strange Phenomena of the Mountain State*. Stackpole Books, 2007.

Windham, Kathryn T. *Ghost in the Sloss Furnaces*. Birmingham Historical Society, 1997.

Zepke, Terrance. *Best Ghost Tales of North Carolina*. 2nd ed. Pineapple Press, 2006.

PHOTO CREDITS

❧ INDEX ❧

Also by Pat Fitzhugh

Visit www.bellwitch.org for more information

CPSIA information can be obtained
at www.ICGtesting.com
Printed in the USA
LVHW090621040520
654930LV00003B/739

9 780970 515650